S0-DNH-104

PEARLMAN MEMORIAL LIBRARY
CENTRAL BIBLE COLLEGE
SPRINGFIELD, MO 65803

Interpreting the Universe as Creation

A Dialogue of Science and Religion

STUDIES IN PHILOSOPHICAL THEOLOGY

Edited by: H.J. Adriaanse & Vincent Brümmer
Advisory Board: John Clayton (Lancaster), Ingolf Dalferth (Tübingen), Jean Greisch (Paris), Anders Jeffner (Uppsala), Christoph Schwöbel (London)

Editorial Formula:
'Philosophical theology is the study of conceptual issues which arise in views of life, in religious thinking and in theology. Such conceptual issues relate to the logical coherence between and the presuppositions and implications of fundamental concepts in human thought, as well as the effects which historical and cultural changes have on these aspects of human thinking.'

1. Hent de Vries, *Theologie im Pianissimo & zwischen Rationalität und Dekonstruktion,* Kampen, 1989
2. Stanislas Breton, *La pensée du rien* (in preparation)
3. Christoph Schwöbel, *God: Action and Revelation* (in preparation)
4. Vincent Brümmer (ed.), *Interpreting the Universe as Creation,* Kampen, 1991

Interpreting the Universe as Creation

A Dialogue of Science and Religion

Editor: Vincent Brümmer

119550

Pharos

Kok Pharos Publishing House – Kampen – The Netherlands

PEARLMAN MEMORIAL LIBRARY
CENTRAL BIBLE COLLEGE
SPRINGFIELD, MO 65803

CIP-GEGEVENS KONINKLIJKE BIBLIOTHEEK, DEN HAAG

Interpreting

Interpreting the universe as creation : a dialogue of science and religion / ed.: Vincent Brümmer. –
Kampen : Kok. – (Studies in philosophical theology ; no. 4)
ISBN 90-242-3207-4
NUGI 631/619
Trefw.: godsdienstfilosofie.

© 1991 Kok Pharos Publishing House, Kampen, The Netherlands
Cover by Rob Lucas
ISBN 90 242 3207 4
NUGI 631/619   W-boek

All rights reserved. No part of this publication may be reproduced, stored in a retrieval system, or
transmitted, in any form or by any means, electronic, mechanical, photocopying, recording or
otherwise, without the prior permission of the publisher.

Contents

Contents

Preface

"We live in an age in which technological developments and scientific discoveries have far reaching effects on our human lifeworld. The demands which life makes on us often seem so strange that we do not know how to cope with them in terms of the usual ways of thinking and value patterns in our culture. The most pressing intellectual challenge of our time is to rethink our usual ways of thought and understanding of the world in order to make these adequate for coping with the changing demands of life with which we are faced today. This challenge is especially urgent for theologians and religious leaders: How can they find ways of conceptualizing the Christian faith which are adequate for making sense of these changes in the demands of life and experience? Christians have always claimed that their faith is eternally adequate for every situation with which life can confront us. If this is so, then theologians cannot afford to ignore the intellectual challenge with which we are all faced in our time. In this situation it is essential that theologians should enter into an intensive and systematic dialogue with the natural and the human sciences in order to gain some insight into the nature of these changes in our lifeworld which the faith is required to address."

These words, taken from the statement of aims of the *Center for Theological Exploration Inc.* in Florida, express the context within which this volume originated. All the papers included here (except for the introductory chapter) were presented at the Second Consultation on Science and Religion which was sponsored by the Center at the University of Utrecht in the Netherlands in December 1990. I would like to express my profound appreciation to the trustees of the Center and to its founder and president Dr. Carl Howie, not only for sponsoring the Consultation but also for providing a generous subsidy making the publication of this volume possible. I trust that it will contribute to the work of the Center which is dedicated to stimulating, sponsoring and coordinating the above mentioned dialogue between theologians and scientists. I would also like to thank the Utrecht Research Institute for Theology and Religious Studies (INTEGON) for hosting the conference, Marc Rietveld and Gerbrandt van Santen for their help in preparing the manuscript of this volume for publication, and last but not least, the various contributors for their very stimulating papers.

Vincent Brümmer

1

Introduction: a Dialogue of Language-games

Vincent Brümmer (Utrecht)

1. *Smothering the Differences*

Religious believers interpret their lives and the universe which they inhabit in the light of their faith. In terms of this interpretation, they ascribe the origin and order of the universe as well as the origin and status of life and of humanity, to the creative activity of God. On the other hand, scientists develop theories in order to explain the origin and the order of the universe and the origin and status of life and humanity. Thus physical cosmologists produce theories like the "big-bang" theory, in order to explain how the physical universe came into being and how it developed the kind of order which it has at present; Biologists try to determine the exact differences between life and organic matter and explain how the former might have arisen from the latter; Psychologists examine the relation between the mental capacities of animals and humans to see how the former might have developed into the latter. How are the claims of the believer related to the theories of the scientist? Do religion and science produce rival explanations of the same phenomena? If so, which explanation is the correct one? Is the doctrine of creation an obsolete religious myth which has now been superseded by the verifiable theories of science? Or does religion provide us with a source of knowledge about the nature of the universe which transcends and extends the range of knowledge which science can provide? Do the scientific and religious pictures of the universe come into conflict or are they in some way complementary? In the latter case, how do they complement each other?

Gilbert Ryle considers the following analogy: "As the painter in oils on one side of the mountain and the painter in water-colours on the other side of the mountain produce very different pictures, which may still be excellent pictures of the same mountain, so the nuclear physicist, the theologian, the historian, the lyric poet, and the man in the street produce very different, yet compatible and even complementary pictures of one and the same 'world'."[1] According to Ryle this analogy is perilous because of the risk involved when we "characterize the physicist, the theologian, the historian, the poet and the man in the street as all alike producing 'pictures', whether of the same object or of different objects. The highly concrete word 'picture' smothers the enormous differences between the businesses of the scientist, historian, poet and theologian... It is these smothered differences which need to be brought out into the open."[2] The same is true when we claim that science and religion provide rival or complementary *descriptions*, or *explanations* of the same phenomena. It is by no means clear that the terms 'description' and 'explanation' are being used in the same sense with reference to the activities of science and religion. Hence, "if the seeming feuds between science and theology or between fundamental physics and common knowledge are to be dissolved at all, their dissolution can come not from making the polite compromise that both parties are really artists of a sort working from different points of view and with different sketching materials, but only from drawing uncompromising contrasts between their businesses."[3]

The same point could be made by claiming that science and religion are neither rival nor complementary ways of dealing with the same issues or even with the same sort of issues. They are rather ways of dealing with very different sorts of issues. Of course, this does not mean that they can have nothing to do with each other. The claims of science and religion can complement each other, or even conflict with each other, not because they provide complementary or rival answers to the same sort of questions, but because they deal with (different sorts of) questions regarding the *same world*. The answers which they provide to their respective sorts of questions might very well involve conflicting presuppositions or implications regarding the nature of the one world in relation to which they are exercising their respective businesses. In order to determine whether this is

---

1.   Gilbert Ryle, *Dilemmas* (Cambridge 1954), 80.

2.   Ryle, 81.

3.   Ryle, 81.

the case, it is essential that we first of all distinguish clearly between these different businesses and try to trace their respective presuppositions and entailments. Let us do this by comparing these 'businesses' with Wittgensteinian 'language-games' and seeing whether we can describe the relation between science and religion as a relation between language-games. How then do the 'language-games' of science and religion differ, how are they related and in what sense is a dialogue between them possible?

2. *Language-games and Forms of Life*

Unfortunately the meaning of Wittgenstein's term 'language-game' is far from clear. As with many other key terms in his writings, Wittgenstein fails to provide a detailed systematic development of it, and his rather cryptic and often aphoristic remarks give rise to extensive speculations and a large variety of proposed interpretations in the Wittgenstein-literature. If we are to employ the term 'language-game' as a tool for distinguishing the activities of science and religion, we will therefore first have to explain the sense in which we are to use it here. Wittgenstein himself defines the term as "the whole, consisting of language and the actions into which it is woven."[4] Thus, language-games are primarily forms of action involving the use of language. For our purposes three aspects are important in Wittgenstein's use of the term: First, Wittgenstein states that his use of the term "is meant to bring into prominence the fact that the *speaking* of language is part of an activity, or of a form of life."[5] Secondly, Wittgenstein remarks that "what we do in our language-game, always rests on a tacit presupposition."[6] Thirdly, Wittgenstein holds that the multiplicity of language-games "is not something fixed, given once for all; but new types of language, new language-games, as we may say, come into existence, and others become obsolete and get forgotten."[7] What does Wittgenstein mean by *forms of life* and by *tacit presuppositions*, and in what sense does he claim that language-games can become *obsolete and forgotten*? Let us take these three points one by one.

---

4. Ludwig Wittgenstein, *Philosophical Investigations*, ed. G.E.M.Anscombe and R.Rhees, trans. G.E.M.Anscombe (Oxford 1953), I.7. (References to part I will be to the numbered remarks, and to part II to the pages).

5. *Investigations*, I.23.

6. *Investigations*, II, p.179.

7. *Investigations*, I.23.

(1) George Pitcher explains the term *form of life* in the light of Wittgenstein's remark that "if a lion could talk, we could not understand him."[8] Of this Pitcher writes as follows: "Suppose a lion says 'It is now three o'clock,' but without looking at a clock or his wrist-watch - and we may imagine that it would be merely a stroke of luck if he should say this when it actually *is* three o'clock. Or suppose he says 'Goodness, it is three o'clock; I must hurry to make that appointment,' but that he continues to lie there, yawning, making no effort to move, as lions are wont to do. In these circumstances - assuming that the lion's general behaviour is in every respect exactly like that of an ordinary lion, save for his amazing ability to utter English sentences - we could not say that he has *asserted* or *stated* that it is three o'clock, even though he has uttered suitable words. We could not tell what, if anything, he has asserted, for the modes of behaviour into which his use of words is woven are too radically different from our own. We could not understand him, since he does not share the relevant forms of life with us."[9] Of course this lion is very different from speaking animals occurring in children's stories. In Kenneth Grahame's *The Wind in the Willows* we can understand the Rat, the Mole, the Badger and the Toad since they do not merely utter English sentences. While doing so, they also behave as Englishmen would do when uttering these sentences, and not like rats, moles, badgers and toads. Clearly then, the meaning of a linguistic expression is its use within the form of life in the context of which it is uttered. Divorced from the form of life, it is meaningless. We can only understand what someone says when we interpret it within the context of the form of life within which it is said. Furthermore, if we were to interpret it in terms of some other form of life, the result would be conceptual confusion. Ryle would say that we are committing a 'category mistake'. Hence his warning referred to above against smothering "the enormous differences between the businesses [or language-games] of the scientist, historian, poet and theologian".

For Wittgenstein religious belief can be viewed as a specific form of life in which people participate. In order to partake in this form of life, we need to be introduced into the language-game embedded in it. According to Wittgenstein this involves learning "the technique of using a picture."[10] It is part of the task of theology to explain this technique to us, i.e. to make explicit the implicit

---

8. *Investigations* II. p.223.

9. George Pitcher, *The Philosophy of Wittgenstein* (Englewood Cliffs, 1965), 243.

10. Wittgenstein, *Lectures and Conversations on Aesthetics, Psychology and Religious Belief*, Ed. Cyril Barrett (Oxford 1966), 63, 71-72.

'conceptual grammar' of the religious language-game. Doing this involves determining the 'logical limits' of the language-game and of the use of the pictures employed in it. If we know the logical limits of the religious language-game, we are able to distinguish it from other language-games and avoid the conceptual confusions which results from 'smothering the differences' between them.

The 'logical limits' to the use of a religious picture has to do with the inferences which can or cannot be validly drawn from it within the religious language-game. I master the technique of using the picture when I know which inferences I can and which I cannot draw from it. Wittgenstein illustrates this point in the light of the 'picture': "God's eye sees everything." Which inferences could a believer draw from this picture, and which inferences would be invalid within the religious language-game? Obviously, a believer would say that, since God's eye sees everything, God is aware of all that happens, not only in the world but also in the hearts and minds of all people: "Almighty God, unto whom all hearts be open, all desires known, and from whom no secrets are hid ..." However, Wittgenstein asks the rhetorical question: "Are eyebrows going to be talked of, in connection with the Eye of God?"[11] Here we have clearly reached the 'logical limits' of the picture. It is conceivable that a child might ask after the eyebrows of God. It is however part of the child's introduction to the religious language-game to learn that such a question is out of order since it transgresses the 'logical limits' of the language-game. For this reason the catechism not only teaches us to give the right answers but also to ask the right questions! There is a second kind of inference which we must also learn to draw if we are to master the technique. Since the religious language-game is embedded in the religious form of life, using the religious picture entails that we commit ourselves to this form of life. Saying 'almighty God, unto whom all hearts be open, all desires known, and from whom no secrets are hid ...', commits the speaker to a complex set of feelings, attitudes and actions. Uttering these words without making the entailed commitment, would be as absurd as the yawning lion who *says* that he must hurry to make his appointment while making no effort to move. Such commissive implications are also an essential part of the conceptual grammar of the religious language-game. Understanding the language-game is only possible if we know how to participate in the form of life in which it is embedded, and if we know how this form of life differs from, and is related to, all the other forms of life in which we might participate.

---

11.   *Lectures on Religious Belief*, 71.

(2) Wittgenstein introduces the term *tacit presupposition* in the context of some remarks on behaviourism in *Philosophical Investigations* (II p.179-180).In these remarks he makes use of the following example: If a doctor hears the groaning of a patient, he *tacitly presupposes* that the groaning is an expression of pain. However, he cannot feel the patient's pain himself. A behaviourist would reject this tacit presupposition as being empirically unverifiable, and would therefore look on the patient merely as an object exhibiting groan-behaviour. This behaviour could be terminated by treating the patient with analgesic. In rejecting the tacit presupposition, however, the behaviourist also takes leave of the form of life of personal relations, since the presupposition is logically constitutive for treating somebody else as a person rather than as an object. Treating somebody else as a person also presupposes that the other is a free agent in the sense of being an originator of his own actions and hence having the ability to have done other than he did.[12] Since this is a counterfactual presupposition, it is also not empirically verifiable: I can only observe what a person does in fact and not that he could have acted differently from the way in which he acted in fact! The determinist who rejects this counterfactual presupposition, also takes leave of the form of life of personal relations, since the presupposition is logically constitutive for this form of life and for the language-game embedded in it. Since such tacit presuppositions are in this way *logically constitutive* for the language-game, they cannot be doubted or denied *within* the language-game itself. Doubting or denying them would entail doubting or denying the language-game as such. In a similar way, P.F.Strawson argues that the presupposition that the material objects which we observe continue to exist at times when there is nobody to observe them, is logically constitutive for the language game of science and of our common sense dealings with the world. The sceptic who doubts this presupposition "pretends to accept a conceptual scheme, but at the same time quietly rejects one of the conditions for its employment. Thus his doubts are unreal, not simply because they are logically irresoluble doubts, but because they amount to a rejection of the whole conceptual scheme within which alone such doubts make sense."[13] Something similar applies to all our illocutionary acts.[14]

---

12. For an illuminating treatment of this point, see Antony Flew, "Freedom and human nature", in *Philosophy* 66 (1991), 53-63. Flew criticises the rejection of this presupposition in the behaviourism of B.F.Skinner.

13. P.F.Strawson, *Individuals* (London 1959), 35.

14. See Vincent Brümmer, *Theology and Philosophical Inquiry* (London 1981), chapter 2.

These too are constituted by presuppositions about the nature of the world. Thus I cannot (logically) make a promise without presupposing that I will be able to fulfill my promise, and I cannot (logically) request someone else to do something while denying that the other has the ability to do what I ask. Making a promise or a request while at the same time denying that the promise or the request can be fulfilled, is as absurd as the lion who *says* that he must hurry to keep his appointment while at the same time continuing to lie lazily in the sun!

As we have shown above, Wittgenstein admits that religious 'pictures' have a commissive force: Using them commits us to a religious form of life. Do they also have a constitive force? Does the language-game of religion require that they should in some way also be claimed to be factually true? According to W.D.Hudson, "what Wittgenstein ... seems at times to have come near to suggesting is that, because religious beliefs have commissive force, that somehow entitles us to by-pass the troublesome problem of their constative force."[15] However, Wittgenstein's remarks on the tacit presuppositions which are constitutive for a language-game, point in another direction. The constitutive presuppositions of a language-game refer to the *factual nature* of the world within which the language-game is to be played. It would be absurd to participate in a language-game without presupposing that the factual nature of the world is such that the form of life to which the language-game commits us and in which it is embedded, can be realized within the world. As we have argued above, commitments are constituted by the presupposition that the factual state of the world is such that these commitments can be fulfilled within the world. That this also applies to the language-game of religious belief, is well illustrated by the following example which is perfectly in accordance with Wittgenstein's views on tacit presuppositions: "If I say 'The Lord is my strength and shield', and if I am a believer, I may experience feelings of exultation and be confirmed in an attitude of quiet confidence. If, however, I tell myself that the arousal of such feelings and confirming of attitude is *the* function of the sentence, that despite appearances it does not refer to a state of affairs, then the more I reflect on this the less I shall exalt and the less appropriate my attitude will seem. For there was no magic in the sentence by virtue of which it mediated feelings and confirmed attitudes: these were *responses* to kind of Being to whom, I trusted, the sentence

---

15. W.D.Hudson, "Some remarks on Wittgenstein's account of religious belief", in G.N.A.Vesey (ed.), *Talk of God* (London 1969), 44.

referred: and response is possible only so long as that exists to which or to whom the response is made."[16]

(3) Although the constitutive presuppositions of a language-game cannot be doubted or denied *within* the context of the language-game itself, this does not mean that the language-game as such is somehow immunized against doubt and rejection. To a greater or lesser extent the forms of life in which language-games are embedded, are all subject to historical and cultural change. Changes in the factual circumstances of our lives and in the problems and demands with which life confronts us, give rise to changes in our culture and thus also to the forms of thought which we find adequate, the language-games in which these forms of thought find expression and in the concomitant beliefs which we hold to be true. The more we become aware of the cultural difference between different times and places, the more we realize the untenability of the platonic view that human thought is essentially timeless and immutable. Because of changes of the demands of life, our forms of thought can never remain adequate for all time. In this sense we can understand Wittgenstein's claim that the multiplicity of language-games "is not something fixed, given once for all; but new types of language, new language-games, as we may say, come into existence, and others become obsolete and forgotten."[17] Elsewhere Wittgenstein illustrates this point as follows: "Earlier physicists are said to have found suddenly that they had too little mathematical understanding to cope with physics; and in almost the same way young people today can be said to be in a situation where ordinary common sense no longer suffices to meet the strange demands life makes. Everything has become so intricate that mastering it would require an exceptional intellect. Because skill at playing the game is no longer enough; the question that keeps coming up is: can this game be played at all now and what would be the right game to play?"[18]

Wittgenstein clearly admits that language-games and the forms of life in which they are embedded, can be contested in the light of the changing demands of life. Since this also applies to religious forms of life, every 'fideistic'

---

16. R.W. Hepburn, "Poetry and religious belief", in A.Macintyre (ed.), *Metaphysical Beliefs* (London 1957), 148. On the constitutive role of factual presuppositions in religious belief, see also my *Theology and Philosophical Inquiry*, chapters 2 and 19.

17. *Investigations*, I.23.

18. Wittgenstein, *Culture and Value* (Oxford 1980), 27. In the *Philosophical Investigations* I.23 Wittgenstein also compares the changes in language-games to changes in mathematics.

8

interpretation of Wittgenstein, like that put forward by Kai Nielsen[19], is excluded at this point. In other words, although religions can be characterised in Wittgensteinian terms as 'language-games embedded in forms of life', this in no way entails that they are self-inclosed autonomous monads which are immune from external criticism[20]. The so-called 'Wittgensteinian fideism' is by no means Wittgensteinian!

Of course not all language-games are to the same extent subject to change.[21] Thus some language-games are so bound up with our lives as personal beings, that they cannot be rejected without giving up all forms of life involving personal relations. Such relations would be impossible without for example such elementary illocutionary activities as making factual assertions, promises and requests and expressing our beliefs, intentions, feelings, expectations, etc. It is hard to imagine the sort of changes in the circumstances of our lives which would make these obsolete. This could only come to pass if all human beings were somehow turned into impersonal robots related to each other causally rather than personally. Although this might be imaginable in science fiction, it as hardly likely in the real world. There are, however, other language-games, including forms of religion, which can become obsolete through changes in the circumstances of our lives. A good example is that of the ancient fertility cults in the Mediterranean basin, which were so strongly embedded in an agrarian form of life, that they could not survive the rise of trade, industry and the urbanisation of life. They proved quite inadequate as means of making sense of these changed circumstances in the lives of people.[22] Other language-games, however, allow for amendment and creative reinterpretation by means of which they can remain adequate to the changing demands of life. To a greater or lesser degree this is true of the traditions of all those world religions which have remained relevant throughout the ages in spite of great changes in the culture and circumstances in the lives of their adherents.

---

19. Kai Nielsen, "Wittgensteinian Fideism", *Philosophy* 42 (1967), 191-209. See also Nielsen's *An Introduction to Philosophy of Religion* (London 1982), chapters 4-5.

20. Fergus Kerr mistakenly rejects "the very idea that religion ... would count as a 'form of life' in Wittgenstein's sense". In this way he tries to avoid applying to religion the fideistic interpretation which he gives to this term in Wittgenstein. See Fergus Kerr, *Theology after Wittgenstein* (Oxford 1986), 29.

21. See Brümmer, *Theology and Philosophical Enquiry*, 63-64.

22. For this example, see H.M. Kuitert, *Wat Heet Geloven?* (Baarn, 1977), 144-145.

This has profound implications for the way in which systematic theology tries to conceptualize the faith. Changes in the demands of life bring about changes in the aspects of faith which are relevant and necessary in order to make sense of life and cope meaningfully with our experience of the world. At different times and in different cultural situations, systematic theology therefore requires different conceptual models in order to highlight those aspects of the faith which are relevant to the cultural and historical situation and to filter out those aspects which are not relevant to the current demands of life. Sallie McFague provides a good example to illustrate this point: "In an era when evil powers were understood to be palpable principalities in contest with God for control of human beings and the cosmos, the metaphor of Christ as the victorious king and lord, crushing the evil spirits and thereby freeing the world from their control, was indeed a powerful one. In our situation, however, to envision evil as separate from human beings rather than as the outcome of human decisions and actions, and to see the solution of evil as totally a divine responsibility, would be not only irrelevant to our time and its needs but harmful to them, for that would run counter to one of the central insights of the new sensibility: the need for human responsibility in a nuclear age. In other words, in order to do theology, one must in each epoch do it differently. To refuse this task is to settle for a theology appropriate to some other time than one's own."[23] Clearly, the task of theology is not merely descriptive, but innovative as well: it should not merely describe the conceptual grammar of a religious language-game, but should also develop innovative proposals which keep the language-game adequate for coping with the changing demands of life.[24]

3. *The Businesses of Science and Religion*

Can these aspects of Wittgenstein's concept of 'language-games' help us in distinguishing and relating the 'businesses' of science and religion? How can we distinguish the roles which science and religion are supposed to fulfil in human life and thought? Let us start with science.

---

23. Sallie McFague, *Models of God* (London 1987), 29-30.

24. Elsewhere I have defended this view on the task of theology more extensively. See my essays on "Metaphorical thinking and systematic theology" in *Nederlands Theologisch Tijdschrift* 42 (1989), 213-228, and on "Philosophical theology as conceptual recollection" in *Neue Zeitschrift für systematische Theologie un Religionsphilosophie* 32 (1990), 53-73.

It could be argued that the aim of science is to develop theories by means of which we can explain, predict and (if possible) control the occurence of factual states of affairs in the world in which we live. Briefly (and greatly simplified), this comes to the following. Scientific theories state the necessary conditions for the occurrence of specific (kinds of) factual states of affairs. Thus they have the form: 'If conditions $A,B,C,D,E...n$ obtain, we can expect state of affairs X to come about'. For example: 'If the switch is turned (and the bulb is in order, the fuse is not blown, the power station is not shut down by a strike, etc. etc.), we can expect the light to go on in the room' or 'If water is heated to 100 degrees celcius (at sea level, and the water is pure, etc. etc.), we can expect it to start boiling'. Such theories enable us to *explain* the occurrence of factual states of affairs (the occurrence of X could have been expected, since $A,B,C,D,E...n$ obtained); to *predict* such occurrences (X will occur whenever $A,B,C,D,E...n$ obtain); and to *control* such occurrences (X can be brought about by causing $A,B,C,D,E...n$ to obtain, and prevented from occurring by preventing any one of these necessary conditions from obtaining). Of course, when such theories enable us to explain and predict occurrences, they do not necessarily also enable us to control these, since we can only bring about or prevent the occurrence of a state of affairs to the extent that it is also in our power to bring about or prevent the necessary conditions for it. Thus explanation and prediction do not necessarily guarantee control.

For our purposes it is important to note one further feature of such theories in science. Each of the necessary conditions for an event, presupposes a further set of necessary conditions, which in turn presuppose further conditions, and so on. The set of necessary conditions which are jointly sufficient for bringing about a state of affairs, is therefore always infinite. For this reason it is in principle impossible to state the logically *complete* set of necessary conditions for an event occurring. Scientific theories therefore merely state the most important conditions and consider the rest to be standing conditions which supposedly occur in any case. Logically speaking, scientific theories have to be qualified by the phrase 'all things being equal': '*All things being equal*, we can expect state of affairs X to occur whenever conditions $A,B,C,D,E...n$ obtain'. Scientific theories are therefore never logically necessary. They always remain hypothetical and subject to empirical falsification. As Karl Popper would say, scientific theories are never more than conjectures which in principle remain open to empirical refutation. Scientific procedures are aimed at testing theories in order to determine the extent to which they are able to resist such refutation.

To the extent that science enables us to explain, predict and control our physical environment, it helps us to cope with the demands with which life and the world confronts us. But more than this is required. It is not enough to know what factual states of affairs we can expect to occur in the world. We must also know what attitude we should adopt and what course of action we should follow in relation to these states of affairs. It is not enough to be able to control events. We should also know to what purpose we should exercise such control. We should not only know what the demands are with which life confronts us, but also how we are to make sense of these demands or how we can ascribe meaning to them. With these questions science cannot help us. Answering them is the business of religions and views of life[25]. As we have pointed out above, religious traditions provide us with conceptual models, or 'pictures' as Wittgenstein would say, in terms of which we can interpret our experience of the world in a meaningful way, and thus make sense of the demands with which life confronts us. The businesses of science and religion are therefore complementary, and both are equally necessary in order to cope with these demands. In this sense it belongs to our human condition to participate in both these language-games. As human beings we need to explain, predict and control our factual environment, and equally to make sense of or ascribe meaning to the demands with which this environment confronts us. Thus it has been and always will be, as long as we humans remain the kind of being we are. Of course this does not mean that the language-games of science and religion are not subject to change. Although people have always tried to explain, predict and control their environment, science has in the course of time developed ever more effective and sophisticated methods for fulfilling these tasks. Although people have always had to make sense of their lives and experience, the conceptual models by means of which they have done so have been changed, amended and creatively innovated in countless ways during the history of every religious tradition. As we have pointed out above, it belongs to the task of theology to develop such creative innovations in order to keep a religious tradition adequate for coping with the ever changing demands of life.

Since science and religion are complementary ways of coping with the same demands of life, they are dependent on each other in many ways. Thus religion is dependent on science in order to know the changing factual environment of which it has to make sense. And science is itself a human activity which as suchis dependent on the conceptual models of a religion or a view of life in order to determine its own sense or meaning. Science and religion can therefore only

25. For a more detailed analysis of the ascription of meaning and of the role of views of life and religions in this regard, see my *Theology and Philosophical Inquiry*, chapters 9-10.

ignore each other to their own detriment. Although the businesses of science and religion are closely related and mutually dependent, it leads to much conceptual confusion if we fail to heed Gilbert Ryle's warning against 'smothering the differences' between them. Science does not provide the means for making sense of the factual environment which it enables us to know, nor does religion provide a theory which enables us to explain, predict or control this environment.

Wittgenstein was very much aware of the conceptual confusion which arises when religious beliefs are interpreted as (pseudo-)scientific theories and religious rituals as (pseudo-)scientific techniques for controlling our environment. Regarding this latter point, he rejects Fraser's account of the African rain-ritual in which gifts are offered to the Rain King at the beginning of the rainy season[26]. According to Fraser, this ritual is a technique by means of which the Rain King is induced to bring on the rain, based upon the primitive hypothesis that it is the Rain King who causes the rain to fall. If this were correct, says Wittgenstein, why do they only perform this ritual in the rainy season when they know that the rain will fall and not in the dry periods when they know that it will not? Obviously such religious practices are ritual expressions of the meaning which the rain has for the believers in the light of their faith in the Rain King, rather than techniques for controlling the rain based upon a hypothesis regarding the Rain King. Scathingly Wittgenstein contends that Fraser can only have put forward such a utilitarian interpretation of religious ritual because of the "narrowness of his own spiritual life" (p.65). His explanation of such religious observances is much cruder than the observances themselves, and he is "much more savage than most of his savages" (p. 68)!

Wittgenstein also rejects the idea that religious beliefs could be interpreted as hypotheses which are open to scientific verification or falsification. Unlike scientific theories which, as we have seen, remain conjectures which are always subject to methodical doubt and empirical refutation, religious beliefs are the constitutive presuppositions of a religious form of life. As such they are not open to doubt or refutation within the context of the form of life itself, any more that the constitutive presuppositions of science are open to scientific doubt or refutation[27]. According to Wittgenstein, the demand that religious beliefs should be subject to empirical verification or falsification, is based upon conceptual

---

26. Wittgenstein, "Remarks on Fraser's *Golden Bough*", in C.G.Luckhardt (ed.), *Wittgenstein: Sources and Perspectives* (Hassocks 1979), 61-81. For this example, see p. 71-72.

27. See note 13 above.

confusion. With reference to father O'Hara's attempt to make religious belief into "a question of science" which can be verified on the basis of scientific evidence, Wittgenstein says: "I would definitely call O'Hara unreasonable. I would say, if this is religious belief, then it is all superstition."[28] The unreasonableness of the demand that religious beliefs should conform to the rules and fulfil the point of scientific hypothese, is well expressed by W.D.Hudson: "But 'How is this religious belief to be empirically falsified?' is a pseudo-problem - like, 'How many runs did Bobby Charlton score in the World Cup?'. And, unless you have decided in advance that cricket is the only game worth playing, the fact that this latter question is nonsensical does not imply that soccer is worthless. Nor does it follow that theological belief is meaningless or disreputable, if it is not a scientific hypothesis. A pro- or anti- apologetic which supposes that it does, is simply wrong-headed."[29]

4. Interpreting the Universe as Creation

How is the way in which religious believers describe the origin and order of the universe and their own place and status within it, related to the things which physical cosmologists, biologists and psychologists have to say about such matters? The papers included in this volume, all deal with various aspects of this question and they all illustrate very well the various points which we have discussed above.

In his paper on "Interpreting the doctrine of creation", Luco van den Brom discusses the nature of the language-game of religion and the role which theological doctrines, like the doctrine of creation, fulfil within it. He shows how different views on the nature of religion, entail different views on the nature of doctrine in general and of the doctrine of creation in particular. This paper prepares the way for the comparison developed in the ensuing papers between the religious doctrine of creation and scientific theories about the universe.

The contributions of Chris Isham and Willem Drees deal with the relation between quantum cosmology and the religious doctrine of creation. Isham's paper provides a detailed discussion of the way in which the creation of the universe is viewed from the perspective of contemporary quantum cosmology. He

---

28. *Lectures on Religious Belief*, 59. See also 57.

29. W.D.Hudson, *Ludwig Wittgenstein. The Bearing of his Philosophy upon Religious Belief* (London 1968), 56.

emphasizes the 'extremely speculative' nature of such cosmological theories, which makes their scientific status a matter for debate. Are we not stretching the concept of 'explanation' in science if it is applied to the origin of everything? How coherent is the claim that science can provide theories about 'everything'? Drees examines the possible points of conflict between quantum cosmology and the religious doctrine of creation. A significant point discussed in both papers is the relation between the concepts of time employed in quantum cosmology and in religious belief. The mathematics of quantum cosmology requires that time be taken as a fourth dimension in addition to the three dimensions of space. Reality is described in terms of a four-dimensional spacetime continuum. Drees points out that this entails a timeless view of reality. In a significant sense, therefore, quantum cosmology appears to be platonistic. Does this not conflict with the concept of time presupposed in religious beliefs about the relation between God and the universe? Drees argues that need not be the case since in the Christian tradition the eternity of God has often been interpreted in terms of timelessness. In this way the concept of time required by the mathematics of quantum cosmology, also seems adequate for the religious doctrine of creation. On the other hand, one could argue that this conclusion 'smothers the differences' between the businesses of science and religion. As we have pointed out above, the meaning of a linguistic expression is its use within the form of life in the context of which it is uttered. It is therefore not necessarily the case that the concept of time means the same in the language games of quantum cosmology and religious belief. Quantum cosmology constructs mathematical models which require time to be described as a dimension analogous to the dimensions of space. But the world described in these mathematical models is not the world in which we as humans live and move and have our being! As G.E.Moore has reminded us, our world is a temporal world in which breakfast is before lunch! If the models of religion are to make sense of *this* world, they must also describe our relations with God in such temporal terms. The concept of time presupposed in quantum cosmology, is not the one which is the constitutive presupposition of human action in the world and of religious models which make sense of such action. Does this entail a conflict between quantum cosmology and religious beliefs about the creation of the universe? Or does it merely point to the conceptual difference between these two language games and the forms of life in which they are embedded?

The papers by Christof Biebricher and Arthur Peacocke compare contemporary biological theories about the origin of life and human consciousness with the religious doctrine of creation. Biebricher argues that, although such theories do not *prove* anything, they nevertheless make it plausible to claim that life and consciousness could have evolved out of inanimate matter. Although biological studies of evolution and the origin of life systematically *disregard* the religious doctrine of creation, they nevertheless do not contradict it. Clearly, this doctrine does not have a role to play within biological theories about the origin of life and consciousness. Its business lies elsewhere. If the nature of the universe is as evolutionary biologists describe it to be, what kind of God must religious believers presuppose if their faith is to succeed in making sense of it? Arthur Peacocke argues that this would require belief in a non-deistic personal God who is intimately involved in all stages of the evolutionary process. Unlike the world of quantum cosmology, the world of biological evolution is fundamentally temporal. For this reason a religious faith which is to ascribe meaning to it, must presuppose a God who can be talked about in temporal terms.

Malcolm Jeeves and Cas Labuschagne discuss the status of humanity in relation to the rest of the universe and especially to the animal kingdom. Jeeves describes recent attempts in psychology and neuroscience to understand the similarities and differences between the mental capacities, and their biological substrate, of humans and of animals, especially those of the higher primates. Such studies show that quantitative differences become so great in some respects that they are most meaningfully described as qualitative differences. Language is a case in point. The differences are therefore sufficient to justify religion ascribing a special significance to human existence in relation to the universe in general and to animals in particular. But what is the special status of human existence according to the Christian faith? In the Christian tradition this question has usually been answered anthropocentrically: The meaning of the universe is determined by the fact that it is the environment for human existence, and the role of humanity in relation to nature is to be the controller of this environment. Humans are called to have dominion over nature. Such views on the relation between humanity and the rest of the universe, have been one of the most important factors leading to the rise of science in western culture. If we humans are to have dominion over nature, we must strive to explain, to predict and to gain control over our natural environment. Cas Labuschagne discusses the significance of humanity in relation to nature from the point of view of biblical studies, and argues that the biblical material should in fact not be interpreted in this anthropocentric way. The conceptual models provided by the Bible are theocentric rather than anthropocentric. They do not justify human dominion which sets humanity apart from nature, but emphasize the fact that the universe as a whole, including humanity, derives its significance from its relation with God.

But why should we (re-)interpret the Biblical message in a non-anthropocentric fashion? In the final contribution to this volume, Martin Palmer argues that the contemporary ecological 'demands of life' make this change more than overdue. The ecological crisis which we are facing today, is not a crisis of scientific resources but a crisis of the mind. It is not the scientific means of control over nature that we lack, but rather the religious models which can change our ways of thinking about our relation to the universe. In the words of Wittgenstein which we quoted above: "Because skill at playing the game is no longer enough; the question which keeps coming up is: can this game be played at all now and what would be the right game to play?" It belongs fundamentally to the language-game of religion to produce the conceptual models in terms of which we can deal adequately with this question.

2

Interpreting the Doctrine of Creation

Luco van den Brom (Utrecht)

1. *Introduction*

Taking the title of this paper for granted we might think that there is a clear-cut conception of the doctrine of creation and it is up to us to determine some possible interpretations. This would not be a too difficult job if we had at our disposal a kind of standard text like a creed, acceptable or meaningful for all of us. In that case, we could discuss the meaning of the different parts of the text and value possible applications of the ideas given in the text. But, do we have a well defined idea of creation? Is there only one established doctrine of creation to interpret? By the way: What do you mean with talk about doctrine in this connection? Is a doctrine of creation like a hypothetical theory in science, open to empirical test? Can we design an crucial experiment to select different candidates for the title of "the doctrine of creation"? This is perhaps a wrong interpretation of the function of a doctrine in the light of modern theological discussions, but the historical conflicts between science and religion were not merely about category mistakes. Therefore, the following questions concern us firstly in this paper: Are we talking about the same issue when we consider (the doctrine of) creation? And: Do we have the same thing in mind when we think about the activity of interpreting such a doctrine?

Some other points concerning the doctrine of creation can be made with the help of some remarks of Rabbi Pinchas H. Peli, a professor in Jewish thought and literature. In the *Jerusalem Post* of October 1987 he wrote an article with an intriguing title: 'To mend the world'. He quotes the Bible: "And God saw every thing that he had made, and behold, it was very good" (Gen.1:31). Peli comments upon this verse: 'But the "good", even the "very good", of the six days of creation was nonetheless not good enough without the additional seventh day, that was "blessed and sanctified." The culmination of creation was not in the "good", but in the "holy". A world without the dimension of the sacred is a world without an inner meaning, without a direction, without higher purpose. The physical universe may be "good" in the sense of the efficiency of a machine that works well and fulfills the expectation of its maker; but, it is not "good" in the sense of not being evil. Physical energy may function, produce, but it does not know how to differentiate between the ethical and the non-ethical, between the meaningful and the meaningless, between bestowing life and blessings or wreaking havoc and disaster.'[1]

In Peli's comments two aspects, central in the concept of creation, are mentioned: the physical and the ethical. Apparently, we make both factual claims and value judgments about the physical universe by calling it a creation. On the one side by talking about the universe as creation we seem at least to suggest that for its existence it depends in some sense on an external factor. Whether this has to do with the genesis of the universe or with its continual dependency is not primarily the issue: the question is whether it is right that the universe itself does not contain the cause for its own existence and is therefore contingent. On the other hand by referring to the universe as a creation we are claiming that it has received from its Creator a meaning which cannot be a conclusion from its internal, empirical structure, and by means of which we can make sense of our life in this universe.

Our first question is now: what is said of the universe when we call it creation? In what sense does the way we think about the nature of the dependency influence and is it itself influenced by our concepts of God and the human being? Secondly, what does the conceptualization of the nature of the dependency tell us about the relations between the Creator and the human creature and between the human and the other creatures? Thirdly, in what sense are both aspects mentioned above related to each other or is it possible to have one of them without the other and to maintain simultaneously that the universe is created? Finally, has a doctrine of creation relevance?

---

1.   Pinchas H. Peli, "To mend the world", *Jerusalem Post International Edition* (Week ending October 17, 1987).

2. About the common object of the doctrine

The word "creation" as it is used in the Bible has a peculiar ambiguity: it can have the character of an primordial event and of a state of affairs. Sometimes it means the act of bringing into existence of something new, but it can also refer to the result or product of that action: e.g. to the world or to specific creatures like animals and human beings. Perhaps these two meanings of the word are merely distinct aspects of the same concept; anyway, this example illustrates that it is reasonable to raise the question: Are we talking about the same matter when we use such words like 'creation' or 'the doctrine of creation'? In our example: When we speak on the doctrine of creation, are we talking about divine agency or in some sense about the universe? And again: are we concerned with a theory of divine agency or of the universe?

In theological handbooks the matter is often presented as "the doctrine of creation of X" whereby 'X' may refer both to a religion, a religious subculture or tradition and to a theologian or a theological tradition. So we can read books on the issue of creation in the theology of Thomas Aquinas or of Karl Barth, but there are also studies on the idea of creation in Jewish or Hindu thought, and e.g. in a lutheran or a calvinistic tradition too etc. These different viewpoints might be presented as competitive options by raising questions like: "Is the Jewish idea of creation more plausible or even more correct than the Hindu one?" or "Is the presentation of the doctrine of creation in Aquinas' theology more convincing than Barth's description?" But again, we are in troubles if we reflect on the notion that we called these view-points "options": options for what? For a theory of divine agency or for a hypothesis about the universe? And if it is a hypothesis, does that mean that a doctrine of creation is like a hypothetical theory in science, open to empirical test?

The presupposition of an option is that there is any problem or difficulty about which human beings are convinced that it need to be solved and that a doctrine of creation could be a serious candidate. It suggests that this concerns situations and events which are describable objectively and independently of our view of life. Therefore, it seems that we, as human beings, are talking about the same issues when we compare those different doctrines and theories. If it is correct that the problem in question is not determined by a view of life, then not only different doctrines of creation are in the competition, but perhaps scientific theories could be reasonable candidates too. It suggests also that by comparing the creational candidates we might have criteria by means of which we can determine the plausibility of any of them. So it is important to have some idea of the sort of the questions which a creational doctrine tries to answer.

Can we give a minimum description of the issues with which apparently every doctrine or theory of creation is concerned? I.e. we are looking for a minimum description which leaves a lot of specifications open because if we specified to much the issues in question, we could rule out several interesting competitors in advance. For instance, we might require that a doctrine of creation informs us on the relation between a transcendental or extra-universal (f)actor and the "big-bang". Such a demand is too strict for several reasons: firstly, it leaves out the possibility that a doctrine could be compatible with such a scientific theory without the necessity of telling us something of such a relation a priori; secondly, it seems to speak with prejudice that you should start an analysis from the point of view of natural science taking its insights for granted; but the other way round is logically not absurd by taking your startingpoint in theology; thirdly, it presupposes that in one or another sense a doctrine of creation should contain references to empirically testable claims and in that sense is like a hypothesis; and just this assumption is open to question; fourthly, it leaves out that the possibility that an concept of creation is not hypothetical at all, but just an attribution of a value to the universe and the life within it. Even if we could specify a relation between an transcendental factor and a big-bang, tomorrow such a explanatory, empirical theory might be obsolete and rendered out of date by new developments. But that does not exclude the possibility that the doctrine of creation is compatible with the new insights too.

Now it seems to be justified to ask: Are there minimum requirements for a doctrine of creation which are general enough to leave some parameters sufficiently unqualified to make it possible to talk about jewish, christian, hindu, even naturalistic etc. conceptions of creation? In a view of life or a religion people are trying to form a clear idea why they are there in this world and why this universe does exist. To discuss questions of why we are there we might expect two types of answers because it is ambiguous what we want to know. Are we looking for a specification of the *complete* set of conditions which explain the existence of the universe necessarily? This is similar to certain aspirations in natural science towards a Unified Theory which might explain everything. Or are we trying to formulate an *intentional* answer for what purpose this same universe is there? In this case we are not interested in answers in terms of conditions which are sufficient as explanation, but in answers in terms of intentions or reasons as *explications* which attribute sense or meaning both to the universe as a whole and to the individual aspects of it. Any of these types of answers - a causal explanation respectively a purposeful explication- should not be precluded a priori, for it is not clear whether or not they are mutually exclusive options. It is not a priori impossible that a Unified Theory is just exactly what God had in mind when creating this world in order to reveal it to the physicists of Cambridge.[2] Religious believers share with their contemporaries the cultural background that contains current beliefs, concepts, theories of the natural sciences and their technical products, etc. Therefore, when they talk about the meaning and purpose of the universe, they cannot ignore developments in scientific insight concerning the existence and origin of the same universe. The meaning and purpose that religious believers attribute to this world may presuppose beliefs about a particular type of universe and these beliefs should be compatible with other (scientific) ideas they have about the same universe. Although the purpose of this world is not derived from its nature, the existence of this particular world is nevertheless a necessary condition for the realization of this purpose. Therefore, a doctrine of creation tells us how the purpose of this world is related to the origin or ground of the existence of the universe.

We can state the minimal requirements for a doctrine of creation now as follows:

1. such a doctrine gives reasons for the existence of the reality or the universe to answer the question: "Why is there something and not nothing?";
2. it describes the degree of dependency of the universe in its relation to a possibly external and sense-giving factor.

Until now we have discussed meanings of the doctrine of *creation* from the point of view of its subject: i.e. the notion of creation by taking for granted the meaning of the term "doctrine". But what do we mean with doctrine? That is the subject of the next section.

3. *Concepts of doctrine*

Do we have the same thing in mind when we think about the activity of interpreting a *doctrine* of creation? What is a doctrine? It is important in this

---

2. See Stephen W. Hawking *A Brief History of Time* (Bantam Press 1988), p.174 about the finding of a physicist's Theory of Everything: 'it will be the ultimate triumph of human reason - for we would know the mind of God.' An answer to this rethorical flourish could be Isaiah 55,8 (N.E.B):
   'My thoughts are not your thoughts,
   and your ways are not my ways.
   This is the very word of the Lord.'

connection to distinguish between religion and theology. Theology is a systematic reflection on religion which in turn is an activity, a practice, a way of life by relating all aspects of the human existence to God, the ultimate source of value and being. A doctrine is the result of theological activity is and as a human intellectual product, it tells us something about the religious way of life, i.e. worship. And what does it tell us?

In his book *The Nature of Doctrine*, George Lindbeck distinguishes three types of theories of religion and relates these with special conceptions of doctrine which play a role in theological discussions.[3]

a) The first type of theory of religion emphasizes the *cognitive* aspects of a religion and stresses that religious expressions primarily function like informative propositions. This view can be called a *propositionalist* one because being religious is understood as adopting a comprehensive set of propositions which describes or depicts the structure of the world in relation to God or to that which is "more important than everything else in the universe".[4] Central to this view is the claim that religious propositions depict the relationship between God and the world in such a way that the picture corresponds with the depicted reality in an *isomorphic* way. This implies an epistemological claim to the truth of the complete set of religious propositions. This claim is based on the truth of propositions derived from experiences of revelation or from biblical texts by way of induction.

In consequence the truth is independent of the utterer. Everyone who has the correct data, is able to discover the truth in the same way as in principle everyone is able to derive the laws of natural sciences from empirical facts. The general framework based on the warrantedly certain facts is certainly true. If we want to criticize such a conception, we can do so because of its apparent foundationalism, but that is out of order now.

In the light of this *propositionalist* theory the cognitive aspects are primary and so religious expressions are seen as describing objective realities and stating facts. If the first order language of the daily religious discourse is cognitive, then the second order language of the systematic reflection on that discourse will have a cognitive character too. Consequently, as product of this reflection, a doctrine can be judged to be true or false: it consists of a set of assertions which may not

---

3. George A. Lindbeck, *The Nature of Doctrine* (Westminster Press, 1984) Ch.1, 2 and 4.

4. See W.A. Christian, *Meaning and Truth in Religion* (Princeton University Press, 1964) p.60.

contradict one another. If doctrines state facts by describing how in reality the relationship between God and the universe is structured, then they are descriptions (or are derived from descriptions) with an empirical content.

In this view doctrinal propositions express a structure which corresponds isomorphically to the structure of the universe in relation to God, otherwise they cannot be objectively true (i.e. independent of the utterer). This implies that at least some propositions can be stated beyond any reasonable doubt and can therefore function as a certain foundation which can be known noninferentially by a human observer - noninferentially because thus any possible bias is eliminated. In relation to our topic there are two basic problems with this conception;
1. an epistemological one: whether such a certain foundation is possible;
2. a logical one: the problem of induction that universal statements cannot be derived from singular data.

This view on doctrine is important to our subject, because here doctrines are treated as hypotheses and seem to be open to empirical test.

b) The second type of theory of religion in Lindbeck's book is the so-called *"experiential-expressivist"* understanding which stresses the experiential dimension of a religion. Being religious is giving expression to an experience that is common to all human beings: a primordial religious experience such as the experience of the mysterium tremendum et fascinans, or the feeling of being absolutely dependent or being grasped by ultimate concern. The experience of the Ultimate is the norm for the expression or the symbolization of the religious belief: it is the immediate cause that leads believers to use symbols which are non-informative expressions for an inner notion of dependency or of a fundamental orientation of life.

There is no logical connection between the ultimate experience and the symbol used for expressing it. There is epistemologically even a parallel with foundationalism: all human beings share the notion of being grasped by ultimate concern and religion is universal in human society. All religions are - as distinguished sets of symbols - expressions of the same core experience.

The difficulty with this view on religion is that you have to accept that looseness of meaning which makes it possible to subsume diverse expressions under one concept. This vagueness makes it impossible to analyze religious statements with respect to their logical structure. Furthermore, apart from the epistemological questions about the apparent common core, there is a semantic problem: How it is possible that the same experience can be given various expressions which contradict one another, and yet retaining its identity?

24

From such a point of view, doctrines are considered as verbal expressions of inner feelings or experiences. In their verbal form they function as symbolisms to pattern attitudes and orientations by the evocation of experiences or behavior, appropriate in the context of a tradition. This evocative function, however, causes many of the ambiguities in doctrines. For different symbols can perform the same function in different settings, but also the same symbol can fulfil very different functions in various contexts. The problem is now whether it is possible in such cases to speak of the same doctrine. This theological approach is not interested in the propositional content of the symbol, but in the question what kind of experience it evokes in its original context and whether it can fulfil the same function in a contemporary situation of a religious community which accepts this symbol. For our subject of discussion, this view on a doctrine of creation is really not interested in any factual claim apart from the believer and his religious context. It is merely interested whether the notion of creation as symbol can evoke experiences or behavior appropriate in relation to the core experience, i.e. being absolutely dependent.

c) A third type of theory of religion, which Lindbeck himself defends, is described as the *cultural-linguistic* approach. The attention is now focused on the respects in which religion resembles language, together with the forms of life involved in each. A religion is seen as a comprehensive interpretive scheme consisting of narratives, legends, parables, myths, rites, and organizing experience, self-understanding and the world in relation to the Ultimate. As framework it organizes the whole of a believer's life and thought, behaviour and experience. It consists of a "vocabulary" as well as a "grammar" determining how to use this vocabulary and how to refer with it, how to say certain things, to see our relations and how to organize our experience.

The external scheme determines the internal religious experience of believers: to be religious is to have appropriated the skill to think, to act, to feel, and to live in the climate of a religious tradition. Although on this view the cognitive aspect is often important, it is not the primary aspect of religion. The primary religious knowledge is not knowledge about what a religion states or denies, but rather knowledge of *how* in a religion the things are said, structured, and estimated. The primary religious language is found in prayer, rituals, praise, hymns, injunctions, sermons, in the use of stories from the Scriptures for self-orientation and meditation etc. The primary religious knowledge is not seen as based on a deep existential experience, but as religious "know-how" that could make such experiences just possible and meaningful.

This implies that a cultural-linguistic approach stresses the self-involving feature of religious language: I cannot affirm "Jesus Christ is Lord" unless thereby accepting Him as "my Lord" and as a consequence accepting a whole way of life. That does not deny the propositional aspect, but this is a characteristic of "*ordinary* religious language when it is used to mold lives through prayer, praise, preaching and exhortation". It is on this level of first-order religious language that human beings linguistically exhibit the truth or falsity of assertions about God and his relations to creatures, their correspondence or lack of correspondence to the Ultimate Mystery. This means that, according to Lindbeck, these assertions cannot be made apart from the religious context, since they have their meaning within the practice of believers seeking to align themselves and others(!) to the Ultimate.[5]

This is a strange restriction for religious utterances, for it implies that religious truth claims are only right or wrong with respect to the religious practice of the speaker or the believer. This ignores the fact that those truth claims concern the way of life and the world of the non-believer as well. Uttering the statement "Jesus Christ is Lord" is certainly a way of aligning the believer with Jesus, but is the claim too that a relation of dependence applies to the lives of non-believers, irrespective of whether it is acknowledged by them or not. Therefore, Lindbeck's cultural-linguistic approach to religion should be *extended* to include not only "vocabulary" and "grammar", but also implicit or explicit religious truth claims. Lindbeck's distinctions are more like the various aspects of religious language in the way that speech acts always fulfil several functions at the same time. Although a speech act may be primarily propositional or expressive or prescriptive, it is never merely one of these at a time. Therefore, an analysis of religious language presents not only the commissive, expressive or prescriptive aspects of a religious speech act, but also its propositional function which concerns the world of both the believer and the non-believer.

In Lindbeck's approach we find a *regulative* view on doctrines. They are understood as rules of discourse, attitude and action, as second-order propositions about how religious language actually works in first-order religious language like adoration, proclamation, prayer and praise. To the extent that religion is an framework structuring experience, self-understanding and the understanding of the world in relation to God, doctrines describe *how* this structuring takes place. So we can say that religious symbols, concepts, rites, injunctions and stories function like a *vocabulary*, whereas doctrines are like a *grammar* which supplies the rules

---

5.   Lindbeck, *Ibid.*, p.69.

according to which we are to use this lexical material and to refer by means of it. On this view doctrine regulates truth claims, but as a rule it does not prescribe what is to be affirmed. Systematic theology is seen as second-order discourse: it does not make ontological assertions but explicates, analyzes and regulates the liturgical, the proclaiming and the moral forms of speech and of action within which ontological assertions are sometimes made. It may be helpful to use a geographic metaphor: a religion is like a map that can be used for guiding belief, speech and action (i.e. the whole life of the believer) by relating it to God. The map tells us *how* to travel, but it is *not* the journey itself. In the same way a religion is a map for the journey of life, structuring it coram Deo, and doctrines are explicitly stated rules for map-reading.

If religion is a map structuring the believer's life, we certainly need rules which tell us how to use the map. However, contrary to Lindbeck, I am of the opinion that the map itself presupposes some ontological claims. It describes relations between elements of the route, but it also shows how it is to be used in relation to some fixed points, (e.g. the north pole) without which the journey could end with the traveler loosing his way. But this presupposes the existence of the north pole, otherwise the map would be useless. Apart from directions for use, we therefore also need some rules of correspondence and these would necessarily entail ontological claims. The analogy with my view on doctrine would be an *extension* of directive doctrines with "pin-pointing" doctrines, which relate the religious map to the reality of our daily life.[6]

Therefore, if systematic theology is a reflection on the utterances of the Christian language using community, this includes a reflection on the status and nature of the apparent truth claims, entailed in the conceptual framework of that community in some specific historical and cultural context. This does not necessarily entail conceptual relativism, provided that we distinguish clearly between the rules, the area of inquiry and the presupposed metaphysics. The rules for making truth claims might also be applicable in a new conceptual framework for the evaluation of the truth value of the assertion. Being dependent on the practice of the Christian faith, systematic theology and doctrine are second-order activities, but this does not justify Lindbeck's claim that they do not make truth claims. On the contrary the truth claims inherent in the assertions of systematic

---

6. In his paper "The Ecological Crisis and Creation Theology", Martin Palmer uses the notion of a *map* which helps us to understand our place and purpose in the created universe. His essay makes clear the *devastating* consequences of neglecting the relevance of the ontological claims presupposed by the map.

theology are derived from the presuppositions and the substance of the claims of the Christian faith.

This more extended view on doctrine is useful for recognizing the different dimensions of e.g. creational language. With this sense of the various religious components of the notion of creation it is easier for us to see that e.g. a doctrine of creation refers to normative aspects and not merely to the apparently ontological ones. Describing self-involving language such a doctrine reveals expressive discourse in so far a religion is world-affirming or world-denying: praising or blaming the Creator. It is not a priori clear how to rank these different aspects with respect to each other. In a propositionalist view this is not a problem: the empirical aspects have the priority above normative implications. In the regulative view on doctrine the evaluation of the components is not determined in advance.

d) In conclusion, interpreting the doctrine of creation is an intellectual activity which presupposes a kind of concept of what doctrines are. That concept determines what kind of questions will be asked concerning a doctrine and its content. In a propositional view a doctrine makes a factual claim which can be discussed in the light of other (i.e. non-religious) knowledge claims we take for granted. In this view it is possible that the evidence of the non-religious propositions is more convincing to the believer and that he might give up his conviction. A good example is the discussion after the publication of Darwin's ideas: a conflict of empirical claims. In an expressivist position we will never have any conflict of this kind; the only possibility of a conflict is that the symbol becomes obsolete and worn out.

In the regulative understanding of Lindbeck the theologian runs away from the conflict which he might observe between religious and non-religious statements, for that view considers doctrine merely as second-order language referring to the religious practice. In my extended regulative view the conflict does not have to be destructive for doctrine, for the rule contains prescriptive and expressive components too. The prescriptive components will be justified by referring to the purpose for which the universe is there; while the expressive components are the human answer in accordance to this purpose. This intentional side of the doctrine of creation can be the reason to rethink the aspects of the conflict in order to see which propositions are denied and which are not. And subsequently they are the reason to look for a possible compatibility of the residue of the propositional content and the prescriptive-expressive elements on the one side and the evidence of the non-religious statements on the other side. This can explain why scientists after Darwin did not give up their religious faith.

4. *Dependency*

At the end of section 2 we state the minimal requirements for a doctrine of creation: it should give reasons for the existence of the universe to answer the question: "Why is there something and not nothing?"; and it should describe the degree of dependency of the universe in its relation to a possibly external and sense-giving factor. In the light of what is said of the several aspects of doctrine in the last section, we can substantiate the guidelines a little bit more. In a doctrine of creation we may expect:

> a. a *prescriptive* element: about the meaning of life (my, our, all life) which is universalized to all forms of existence (material and/or spiritual) by relating them to the value of the Ultimate (F)Actor, i.e. God;
>
> b. an *expressive* element: about a doxology on the Source of existence and value in a world-affirming faith; or about denunciation and lamentation in case of a world-denying belief;
>
> c. a *propositional* element: about dependency explicated in terms of the relation between freedom and causality; central themes are divine causality resp. agency; and divine agency as empirical influence and/or inspiration and human freedom.

The prescriptive and expressive constituents are interrelated e.g. in so far the prescriptions express the approval of the Ultimate Value. But what about the next question: In what sense is the propositional one related to the other ones? What is said of the universe by calling it creation? In what sense is the way we think about the nature of the dependency influenced by our concepts of God and the human being and vice versa? To answer those questions is a tough job for several monographs; therefore I confine myself to a short systematic survey of classical, theological conceptions of universal dependency in order to see the function of the concept of God and the human in it.

For a description of relations between God, the world and the human being we can distinguish the various conceptions according a degree of union or fusion. On one side of the scale God, the world and the human being are considered as unity, whereas on the other side they are regarded as having a maximum of individual autonomy. These points on the scale are traditionally dubbed as "pantheism" and "deism"; in the first view God is considered as immanent in the world, whereas in deism He is thought as wholly transcendent. Between them the several forms of theism (and panentheism) are located which attribute God an absolute autonomy, but the world and the human beings a relative one. In pantheism God, the world and the human beings form a whole system which does not leave the constituent elements any freedom: they are determined in their relations and inner structures. In deism the world has a certain independent existence and human beings have a relative freedom to determine their own way of life within certain limits.

With these general distinctions in mind we can describe various forms of the doctrine of creation. In a *pantheistic* tradition creation is seen as a process of emanation: this world is growing or grown out of the godhead and is therefore divine in its nature. As part of this created world the human being participates in this divine character, but the nature of this divine character may take various forms. This depends on the way the relation between the Divine Being and the universe is seen.

In a naturalistic pantheism like Spinoza's there is no substantial difference between God and the universe: there is only one substance. And all relations internal in this substance are of a logical character: the order of things is geometrically perfect. This means that what we call causality in daily life is in fact logical coherence. In this view the human being is completely determined and there is no freedom of God in the creative system either. The universe runs absolutely unerringly on its rails. The prescriptive element in this view states that human persons accept their place in this *perfectly* ordered system. But there are other types of pantheistic thinking: e.g. Schleiermacher's theology which denies a substantial distinction between God and the world and prefers monism to dualism. In Hegel's philosophy the freedom of the human agent is stressed whereas the godhead is inherent in the history of mankind and nature is spirit not yet aware of itself but contributing to the development of the Absolute Spirit. Here the relations are considered in a more organic way and it leaves room for talk about the world as God's embodiment. In the latter types of pantheism time is an aspect of the universe, whereas in the naturalistic type it should be an illusion, because of the logical structure of reality. If time is a real aspect, the human being can be an agent and history is real and so the Absolute Spirit can develop itself.

What is shown with these examples is that interpretation of the doctrine of creation does *not* take place *apart* from the rest of what is believed, but is dependent on the background or framework of other convictions and opinions. Interpretation appears to be the activity to make sense of a doctrine in the light of broader framework. The same sort of things can be said of *deism*. In this view the emphasis is on the perfection of God as agent who creates the world as a perfectly running machine: a clockwork universe which needs no intervention or help of God. Above the accent is on the human freedom and responsibility and therefore the doctrine of creation will be interpreted in such a way that human freedom is respected.

So, in deism, God as perfect Creator is in retirement; perhaps his only job might be the inspiration of the human agents with a regulative ideal. And if we have the augustinian problem about the moment of creation ("Is there time before creation?"), a deist might say: "The universe is an eternal gift, for God is eternally creator." In this case we see an ontological dualism: two eternal entities, only one is necessary for the existence of the other which in turn is contingent.[7] This deism is world-affirming and stresses the responsibility of the human agent for what happens in human history. But there was an world-denying ontological dualism which rejected God the Creator because of the notion that being embodied is similar to being in prison or being degraded. God the Creator is blamed for his action and another Deity is praised as the Supreme God of Love who liberates human beings from enslavement to the body. This type of ontological dualism presupposes two deities as explication of the existence of the world and the problem of evil on the one side and the positive value of the bodily death as liberation. Here again, we see the broader doctrinal framework functioning as background in the interpretation of the doctrine of creation.

In a theistic framework the accent is on a personal interaction between God and the human beings. We may expect that in this context a doctrine of creation is interested in those things which make such interactions possible. God is regarded as being absolutely autonomous and not dependent for any action on anything else. This is expressed in the classical formula: *creatio ex nihilo*; this means that there is basically one source which permits all beings their existence. God is not determined by an external factor like a second godhead or preexistent matter or as factor in a logical coherent system. He is merely determined by Himself, i.e. by his own will.

In deism creation ex nihilo is a possibility too, but the intention in deism is different from the one in theism. In deism the created world is, so to say, put in the hands of the human beings and their responsibility: and the Lord "let the vineyard out to vine-growers and went abroad." In *theism* the created world is put in the hands of the same beings but now in order to live coram Deo (in relation to God; in God's presence). The created world is not merely a gift but the place for the *history of God and the human beings*. This can be seen in the distinction in Trinitarian theology between the immanent and the economic Trinity: the

---

7.   There is also neutral ontological dualism which is defended by Aristotle: the Creator or Demiurge forms already available matter. Both Creator and matter are necessary for the existence of the cosmos.

notion of the immanent Trinity stresses divine autonomy and that of the economic Trinity concerns the involvement of God('s history) in human history. Therefore, Christian Trinitarian theology will place extra emphasis on the reality of time as a necessary condition for the possibility of history.[8] So a doctrine of creation in a theistic framework is not primarily interested in a set of hypotheses about how precisely it was possible that this world came into existence. It tries to tell us the reason why this is the case in order to prescribe a kind of attitude and behavior towards God as the present Source of this reality. Here we recognize the regulative character of this doctrine in a theistic framework: it is the broader background of intentions formulated in other doctrines that determines the interpretation of the doctrine of creation. It is because of this reason that theism has a flexibility towards the results of the natural sciences: not a technical explanation - how all has happened - is the ultimate belief, but the explication of the intention - why it has happened.[9]

5. *Intention and meaning*

Intention plays a key-rôle in the argumentation that the doctrine of creation is more than a set of propositions or factual claims. That an event or a state of affairs expresses an intention or a meaning or a message, is not a deduction or inference on the basis of the factual description. The intention cannot be reduced to the factual depiction of the situation although to express intentions cannot be done without something that fulfills the rôle of a medium. We might express our feelings e.g. in a letter to let them be known to our friends: our emotions are not of the same nature with the used paper and ink. But, if we want to express them, we need to perform some action.

Similarly, talk about the question why the universe is there, is not primarily a discourse about the factual ingredients of the cosmos but about the sense or meaning expressed by its existence in this way and not in any other. Recognizing this meaning and subsequently assenting to it implies the acceptance of the intention as basic for our way of life. Assenting that the world is created to make

8. Therefore, the physicist's notion of the indistinguishability of space and time, which suggests a platonic or timeless universe, is at odds with a Trinitarian theology.

9. See section 2.d; also Chris J. Isham's paper "Quantum Theories of the Creation of the Universe", p.39; and Christof Biebricher's paper "Evolutionary Research", p.99.

a personal relation between God and the human being possible is a shift from recognizing the relatedness of the creature and his Creator to experiencing the personal relationship. In other words it concerns the appreciation of the value of the relatedness as medium and ground for the personal relation. In the words of the Christian tradition: the creation in the sense of the created world is appreciated as the place for the covenant. Reality is not an accident and life is not a bad dream but in such framework they have purpose.

Since the created world is the place for the covenant, the interaction and the cooperation of God and human beings, a doctrine of creation has to consider the status of space and time. Both space and time are constitutive for the possibility of agency and, therefore, for history. When the created universe is spatial and/or temporal, a doctrine of creation seeks to answer the following question: Are space and time (or spacetime) creatures or characteristics of the created order; or do they also apply to God as the Ultimate Agent? From the point of view of a Trinitarian theology, the reality of the historical development of the personal relationship between God and human beings, is necessary because of the presence of Jesus Christ in history. But, simultaneously, it seems to be incompatible with the kind of timeless universe presupposed in modern physical cosmology. Thus it is relevant for a Trinitarian theology to reflect on the meaning of the concept of 'time' which is often used in modern physics, as far as this is part of the contemporary cultural background. It is a problem for Christian theology if it has to explain the relation between God and the created world (including humanity) as a history of a reciprocal interaction in a modern culture which seems to deny the reality of time at a fundamental level. Thus the systematic theologian has to examine the ontological status of the concept of time in physical theories.[10]

From a philosophical point of view the meaning of the concepts of space, time and spacetime varies with the different theories which interpret them.[11] According to the relational theory of time, events are more fundamental than moments, since moments are classes of simultaneous or co-existent events. These classes can be ordered by the most fundamental relation of *before-and-after* and

---

10. From this point on, my paper is largely devoted to comments on the contributions of Chris Isham and Willem B. Drees. If the reader so wishes, he could return to these comments after having read the papers of Isham and Drees.

11. The idealist, the realist or absolutist, and the relational theories of space and time are the most important. See e.g. I. Hinckfuss, *The Existence of Space and Time* (Oxford University Press, 1975); P.J. Zwart, *About Time: A Philosophical Enquiry* (N.H.P.C., 1976); G.J. Withrow, *The Natural Philosophy of Time* (Oxford University Press, 1980); R. Flood and M. Lockwood ed. *The Nature of Time* (Blackwell, 1986).

time can be defined as the *generalized relation of before-and-after extended over all events*. Because, in my opinion, the relational theory of time is the most plausible, I agree with Chris Isham's remark that time can be thought of as an *internal* property of a system[12], and also that time can be visualized in spacetime diagrams. But I disagree that this allows us to *define* time in spatial terms (like the position of the hands of a clock, the radius of a circle or the volume of an expanding universe).[13] Of course, we might employ the value of these variables as a measure for timekeeping, but such a value does not *define* the characteristics of time. Isham's statement that "the position of the hands of a clock does not measure time - it *is* time" would imply that there are as many kinds of time as there are sorts of clocks. However, a clock tells us what time it is, but not what 'time' means, because the 'variables' of the clock (e.g. its hands) presuppose the possibility of change, and therefore time itself. In an operational definition like Isham's, we can use the notion of a clock to describe what we mean by 'time' in a specific (quantum) context, but that description cannot define the characteristics of its own presupposition.[14] It is doubtful, therefore, that we could generalize physical concepts as if they were to prescribe the only possible ontology. For this philosophical reason a theological notion like Gods action in history is not *a priori* meaningless because of a "spatialized" concept of time in modern physics.

Like 'time', the concept of space is also constitutive for agency and the theologian may raise the question whether creation took place "in" or "with" space. Creation with space would mean that space is given with the creation of the world, so that it can be called an internal property of the system of the universe. In this case God would be a spaceless Creator. But can we make sense of spaceless agency? Some theologians could not do so and therefore suggested that we conceive of God's creative action as making room for creatures in his own space.[15] Elsewhere I suggested that we can imagine that the three-dimensional space of the created cosmos is part of higher dimensional system of

---

12. According to a relational theory, this can also be said of space.

13. See Isham's paper "Quantum Theories", p.47-52.

14. Isham's objection that we cannot presuppose an absolute background time like in Newtonian physics, does not apply in a relational theory in which we can define a process as being a clock with which to measure the before-and-after relation.

15. See Karl Heim, *Christian Faith and Natural Science* (Harper and Brothers, 1953); Karl Barth, *Church Dogmatics* II/1 §31, III/1 §41; Jürgen Moltmann, *God in Creation* (SCM Press, 1985), Ch. VI.

divine space. This model of higher dimensionality could enable us to talk about the notion that God transcends the three-dimensional space of material entities and is active in it without being contained by it. Because of the logic of the Anselmian conception that God must be thought of as "a being than which nothing greater can be conceived", divine space possesses an infinite number of dimensions.[16]

This model is criticized by Willem Drees as follows.[17] Firstly, the fact that the velocity of light is finite might create a problem in God's internal information system: He could not be informed about the more outer regions of his own space. Secondly, Divine spatiality would imply that the distance between the different parts of his extended existence will vary. Finally, consistent cosmological theories seem to restrict the number of dimensions because of the specific nature of physical problems (like in superstring theory). This critique deals with theological and physical statements as though they were on the same level and, moreover, the physical has priority over the theological. Only those theological propositions seem to be acceptable that are in *physical* sense compatible with contemporary scientific insights.

However, my theological proposals are not meant to solve physical problems at all, but seek to cope with some theological issues about Divine agency and transcendence. It is precisely the notion of Divine transcendence that is neglected by raising such physical questions about God's spatiality as Drees does. God's world is not this created world writ large: although we use the same concept of space in the model of God's higher dimensional agency, that does not imply that the content of the space of the creatures is the same as that of the Divine space with the same natural laws and the same fundamental constants. The reason is simple: theology is not physics! Drees' alternative God-conception - a transcendental regulative ideal - seems to take leave of Divine agency and, therefore, cannot answer the question "Why is there anything at all?". A higher dimensional model avoids pantheism and can account for a intentional description of our created world.

---

16.   See my "God's Omnipresent Agency", *Religious Studies* 20 (1984), pp.637-655.

17.   See Willem B. Drees' paper "Potential Tensions between Cosmology and Theology", §4.3.

6. Relevance of the doctrine of creation

Is the doctrine of creation relevant or is it ornamental? In biblical theology the notion of creation is often presented as backwards projection. Central in the message of the Bible is the history of God and his people and the idea of creation is more like a footnote of this history. A footnote is not a fundamental part of the content of the text: it tells us "By the way, *our* God created the world and the gods of other people do not." Original or not, the biblical notion of creation functioned in a confrontation with other beliefs like the babylonian religions to answer questions about what counts as basis of human life in that time. The doctrine of creation is relevant in our time, perhaps more than in the time of the Old and New Testament because of ultimate claims of some scientists on the one side and the fact that science became an integral part of our life-style or way of life. This means that it is part of the religious framework which is the background in the interpretation of doctrines. And science speaks about the world which in the doctrine of creation is called a created reality. Its scientific results and the technological possibilities confronts us with the normative question what to do. As long as it is impossible to derive norms from facts a doctrine of creation in its regulative function is important. Therefore we need at some level coordination of science, religion and theology.

3

Quantum Theories of the Creation of the Universe

Chris J. Isham (London)

1. *Introduction*

(1) The big-bang: A major motivation for trying to construct a theory of the quantum creation of the universe (QCU) is the substantial observational evidence that we live in an expanding universe in which each piece of matter is moving steadily away from every other. When extrapolated backwards, this motion suggests that at about 15×10^9 years ago the material content of the universe was compressed into a tiny region from which it expanded at great speed against the force of gravity. Such a behaviour is consistent with the theory of general relativity. However, general relativity also implies that the original configuration must necessarily have been a point at which the mathematical structure of the theory breaks down. This removes any possibility of extrapolating the behaviour of the system to before this event, and thus it is as if the universe began at some finite time in the past - a situation that raises intriguing scientific and philosophical questions.

Of course, this observation is very speculative and one might conceive of a number of modifications to general relativity which avoid the singularity. However, theories of QCU do take seriously the idea that there is some real sense in which the universe began around 15 thousand million years ago. The challenge is to ascribe scientific meaning to this statement and, in particular, to the associated concept of the beginning of time.

The central question therefore is whether this coming into being of the universe can be explained, or at least described, using the methods of theoretical physics. If the answer is no - it is impossible as a matter of principle, then we are faced with a fundamental limitation on the applicability of physical science, and it is pertinent to ask whether this has any philosophical or theological significance. For example, one might be tempted to invoke a God-of-the-gaps who performs a Deistic creation of the universe at the precise point where the theories break down. Such a step is psychologically understandable even if it is not justified logically. On the other hand, if the answer is yes - we can describe the origination event in scientific terms, then it is again reasonable to ask whether such a striking claim has any non-scientific significance. Stephen Hawking certainly thinks so. In his famous book[1] he seems to imply that the construction of such a theory would form a substantial step towards knowing the mind of God!

For many years following the initial development of the big-bang model of cosmology, the negative answer was deemed to be the correct one. However, within the last 10-15 years the situation has changed dramatically and much effort has been directed towards the goal of constructing a genuine theory of the origination[2] of the universe in which the addition of quantum ideas to general relativity plays a central role. In assessing these ideas it must be emphasised that:

1. There is more than *one* scheme of this type.

2. None of them are *proper* theories, even within their own terms. They are at best hints of how a genuine origination theory might one day be constructed.

3. Theories of this type are *extremely* speculative and have nothing like the same scientific status as, say, ordinary atomic physics or even the more exotic branches of modern elementary particle physics or astrophysics. It would therefore be a mistake to pay too much attention to the details of any particular scheme. On the other hand, the various suggestions that have arisen do have certain ideas in common which are themselves of considerable philosophical

---

1.   S.W. Hawking, *A Brief History of Time* (London 1989).

2.   In a personal letter, the philosopher Adolf Grunbaum objected to my use of the word creation in an earlier paper (C.J.Isham, Creation of the Universe as a Quantum Tunneling Process in R.J. Russell, W.R. Stoeger & G.V. Coyne (eds.), *Physics, Philosophy and Theology: A Common Quest for Understanding* (Vatican City 1988). His grounds were that it tends to suggest a necessary creator, and, in much of what follows, I will adopt his suggestion of using the more neutral word origination. See also A.A. Grunbaum, "The pseudo-problem of creation in physical cosmology", in *Philosophy of Science* 56 (1989), 373-394.

interest (for example, the issue of the beginning of time), and there must surely be something of theological relevance in the fact that it is now deemed to be possible, at least in principle, to construct a scientific explanation/description of the origin of the universe.

(2) What is a creation theory?: In posing this question I am seeking to elucidate what the physicists who work in this field mean by a creation theory and, in particular, what distinguishes such a theory from any other piece of theoretical physics.

A minimal requirement is to provide a mathematical description of the origination event that is free of the singularities that arise in classical general relativity and which gives a satisfactory meaning to the notion of the beginning of time. A far more ambitious aim is to provide a theoretical structure that predicts a *unique* universe. Thus, such a theory would say:

1. what *type* of matter (particles, fields or whatever) is present in the universe,

2. how *much* of it is present at any given time,

3. what it is *doing* at any given time,

all of which should potentially be related in some way to the origination event.[3] But note that the one question which even a very ambitous creation theory cannot address is "Why is there anything at all?". That is strictly a job for the theologians! (In this context note the fundamental contrast between the three scientific requirements of a creation theory and the two requirements for a doctrine of creation cited in Luco van den Brom's article.)

Of course, one crucial scientific question is: "Predict in terms of *what?*"; that is, what *assumptions* are fed into the theory from which the desired results are to be obtained? In discussing this issue it is helpful to look at the art of theory construction from a perspective that dominates much work in this area. This is the desire to satisfy certain general theoretical principles. It is *not* derived from any particular experimental or observational results - not even the existence of the big-bang.

For a creation theory, the basic requirement is that of quantum gravity in general, which is to reproduce classical general relativity and normal quantum

---

3. One must not be prejudiced in advance about the meaning of the word event. It is a convenient term for referring to the processes at work in the origination, but it must not be taken too literally, particularly in regard to its usual temporal connotations.

theory in their appropriate domains. An important role is played by the *Planck length* L_P defined to be $\sqrt{(Gh/c^3)}$. This has the dimensions of length and a value of 10^{-35} metres. Here G is Newton's constant (which sets the scale of gravitational effects and is therefore a key constant in general relativity), h is Planck's constant (which sets the scale of quantum effects) and c is the speed of light. The associated *Planck time* $t_P = L_P/c$ has the value 10^{-42} seconds. These - minute quantities determine the regimes in which quantum gravity effects are expected to become highly significant. Thus the minimal requirement for a theory of quantum gravity is that it reproduces classical general relativity and conventional quantum theory at scales significantly larger than these characteristic values.

One may be able to find several theoretical structures that satisfy these primary input requirements, and each of these theory types may in turn admit a number of concrete examples of a theory. Finally, each such specific theory will generally admit a large number of solutions that are typically specified by *boundary conditions* of one sort or another.

In an origination theory these different solutions would correspond to the set of all possible universes (and their time evolutions) that are compatible with the particular theory. A complete origination theory would be one in which there is only *one* (presumably very complicated) solution, corresponding to a unique universe.

(3) How does a creation theory compare with a normal piece of theoretical physics?: In the light of these remarks we can now consider the requirements listed above for a full origination theory, starting with the *type* of material present. One of the striking features of modern physics is the way in which a few basic requirements can restrict considerably the sort of entity that can exist. For example, the internal spin of a quantum mechanical particle moving in three dimensions is necessarily an integral multiple of $1/2h$. Thus if we seek to describe a particle of, say, spin $3/4h$ we can assert with confidence that *no* framework consistent with quantum theory could yield such a particle.

The ideal situation for an origination theory would be if the primary requirement of compatibility with classical general relativity and normal quantum theory is such that it can be satisfied by only one specific theory in one theory class. This theory would then lead to a definite prediction of the types of entity that can exist.

For example, in recent years, superstring theory has been widely acclaimed as affording a consistent reconciliation of quantum theory and general relativity. However, no one has yet constructed a QCU theory based on superstrings.

Indeed, the thrust of recent ideas has been more towards the assumption that the techniques which have been developed for handling the origination event (and hence the beginning of time) could be adapted to any unified theory of matter that might emerge from the researches of particle physicists. In particular, the creation theories do not depend in any fundamental way on the details of what type of entity is present. Thus, from this perspective, the current theories of QCU do not offer anything over and above what is already contained in modern elementary particle physics.

The situation in regard to *how many* of each type of entity is present is strikingly different. In most branches of physics the number of objects being investigated is potentially at the disposal of the experimenter, and it is therefore important to emphasise that one of the main predictions of a complete QCU is precisely the amount of matter that is present at any given time (within the general probabilistic constraints of quantum theory). More specifically, one aspires to construct a *unique* quantum state for the universe. The techniques employed for handling the origination event achieve this by effectively imposing boundary conditions that select one particular state from the large number which would otherwise be available to the quantum theory.

The prediction of what the universe is *doing* at any given time is also an important ingredient of a complete creation theory. In most branches of theoretical physics the question of how the system is behaving in time is grounded in a basic dualism between the equations of motion, which describe all *possible* motions of the system, and the boundary conditions, which determine the *actual* motion of any particular system. For example, if I throw a piece of chalk across a lecture room it could move along a number of possible trajectories, all of which satisfy Newton's second law of motion (mass x acceleration = force applied). However, the actual path followed by the chalk is determined by the position of my hand when I release it and the velocity which I impart to it.

This analysis can be extended to a Newtonian universe as a whole and shows that the positions and velocities of the particles at any particular time are uniquely determined by their values at any earlier (or later) time.[4] Thus the equations of motion only yield *conditional* histories: they give the state at any time in terms of the state at some other time, but that is all. To produce a creation theory in this framework it would be necessary to argue that, for

---

4.　Modern ideas of chaotic motion have shown that this statement needs to be expanded somewhat. The ensuing subtlety is not directly relevant here but nevertheless it is something that should be kept in mind when talking about determinism in classical physics.

example, there is some special fiducial time (perhaps the big-bang) at which the state of the universe can be specified in a way that is mathematically simple but which nevertheless leads to the complex world we see around us today. But this does not seem very plausible since one expects some sort of conservation of complexity to apply to the deterministic evolution of a classical system.

Similarly, the field equations of general relativity possess many solutions which describe a universe emerging from an initial singularity. These are all possible histories for the universe, but the theory cannot select any particular one. The Deistic solution to this problem is to ascribe to God that role of setting the initial conditions which, in the case of the piece of chalk, is played by my hand and my will that moves it. The QCU solution is to fix the initial conditions in the quantised theory in some natural way. We will see later how this might be done.

2. *Quantum Creation in a Fixed Spacetime*

The instinctive picture of space possessed by most people is of a big box which contains the matter in the universe. Thus it is understandable that the first serious theories of the origination used a mathematical framework in which space and time form a fixed background and in which matter is created at some specific point in the corresponding spacetime. This is illustrated in Figure 2.1 where the lines moving away from the origination point are the world-lines of the created particles. A point on the world line specifies the position in space of the particle at the corresponding time (the value along the vertical axis). Thus each world line represents the entire history of the particle from its moment of production. Note that I have had to drop the third spatial direction in order to draw the (essentially four-dimensional) diagram on a piece of paper.

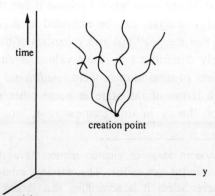

Fig. 2.1 Creation in a Fixed Spacetime

There is a sense in which theories of this type can be said to involve the idea of 'creation from nothing', but what is created is only the material world. Space and time themselves are eternally pre-existent and the 'nothing' from which the world emerges is empty space, viz. 'no thing'.

The obvious question to ask of such a theory is what happens to the conservation of energy? The initial prognosis for satisfying this universal requirement is not too promising. The rest-mass energy ($E=mc^2$) and kinetic energy of the created matter are both positive, whereas it can be plausibly argued that the energy of empty space ('no thing') is zero (what else could it be?). However, as Tryon[5] pointed out, see also the article by Willem Drees, every piece of matter in the universe attracts every other piece gravitationally, and the potential energy of this attraction is always negative (because energy has to be expended in separating matter against the force of gravity). Thus the possibility arises that this negative gravitational energy might cancel the positive rest-mass energy of the matter in the universe, and various detailed arguments (with various degrees of plausibility) have been proposed purporting to show that this is indeed so. The picture that emerges is thus one in which empty space is potentially unstable to the production of matter, since the total energy of both is zero!

It is not possible to construct such a creation theory within the rigid deterministic framework of classical Newtonian physics, but the introduction of quantum ideas changes the situation. In practice, theories of this type have involved some sort of nucleation process in which a minute particle of matter is produced at some time. This then generates a zero-energy conserving, fire-ball explosion, and this is what we call the big-bang.

This picture is attractive but it is subject to several serious objections. For one thing, the observational evidence is that every piece of matter in the universe is moving away from every other piece, *not* from some fixed point in space. However, even if this defect is overlooked there are still several major difficulties, one of the most crucial of which is to decide what determines the time at which the initial nucleation occurs.

The difficulty is that, within an infinite, pre-existent, and homogeneous timeline, there is simply no way whereby the mathematics can select one particular time for the creation event. Similarly, there is no way of picking a particular spatial point for the creation. Instead, theories of this type are prone to predict a creation at every time or, to be more precise, as quantum theories they predict a non-zero *probability* of creation within any finite time interval with the

---

5.   E.P. Tryon, "Is the universe a vacuum fluctuation?", in *Nature* 246 (1973), 396.

origination points being distributed in space. This leads at once to an infinite number of creation events within the background spacetime. One obvious difficulty with this picture is that the material emerging from one creation point can cross that associated with another, and we do not see anything like this happening!

This problem is a fundamental one and has resulted in physicists trying to produce theories in which time and space are themselves created in some appropriate sense. Such a move has interesting historical precedents. The impossibility of determining the actual instant of creation was invoked by Kant in proving the first half of his antinomy that (i) the world began a finite time ago, and (ii) it did not do so. The same problem had been considered earlier by Augustine who concluded that space and time should be considered as *relations* within the natural order, and hence themselves come into being at the moment of creation. One is also reminded of those versions of the creation myth involving the separation of Earth and Sky, in which 'space' is identified as the separating agent.

Note that, since quantum theory deals only with the *probability* of events occurring, prior to a Tryonic creation the theory could at best be said to describe the 'potentiality' or 'latency' of the event. This accords rather nicely with the old Greek idea of chaos as the yawning abyss of infinite empty space which contains only the potentiality of being. Thus the scientific move away from theories of this type to those in which space and time are also created, mirrors the construction by early Christian theologians (such as Augustine) of the *creatio ex nihilo* doctrine in which the Greek concept of a demiurgic creation from potential being was replaced by the idea of God's creation from total non-being. From a scientific perspective, this requirement leads naturally to general relativity and, ultimately, to the modern quantum theories of creation.

3. *Space and Time in General Relativity*

To speak of the 'creation' of time sounds like a contradiction in terms. After all, 'create' is a verb and hence its use would appear to be meaningless if there was no time at which the act of creation was in the present, not to mention earlier times in which it lay in the, as yet unrealised, future. However, it is important to realise that the Newtonian/Kantian picture of a transcendent space and/or time has been largely abandoned by 20th century physics and replaced with a more fluid image in which the structure of spacetime is as much fair game for the investigations of experimental physicists (or the fantasies of theoreticians) as is the matter contained therein. Of particular relevance in this respect is the theory of general relativity, to which we now turn.

(1) Curved spaces: The basic idea of general relativity is that the three-dimensional space in which we live is *curved*. The deviation from flatness at any particular point is regarded as being a measure of the strength of the gravitational field at that point, and this can change in time. In the context of big-bang cosmology, the reason why the galaxies appear to be moving apart from each other is not because they were all created at some time in the past (as in Figure 2.1) but rather because they are embedded in a closed, curved space whose size is increasing with time.

The curvature of a space is described mathematically by deviations from the Pythagoras theorem. Taking again a two-dimensional example, the lengths of the edges of a right-angled triangle in a flat space satisfy the well-known relation $x^2+y^2=s^2$ where s is the length of the hypotenuse. But now imagine trying to draw the same triangle on the curved surface of a ball. It is clear that the hypotenuse is smaller than it is in a flat space, and hence the Pythagoras relation is no longer satisfied. This idea generalises easily to the more physically relevant case of a three-dimensional space, and the deviations from the usual Pythagoras-theorem are coded mathematically into the so-called components of the metric tensor which can vary from place to place in the space. The famous Einstein field equations are a set of equations that determine the ways in which these metric components can change in time.

(2) Spacetime Diagrams: An important role in general relativity is played by spacetime diagrams. In order to draw such things on a piece of paper it is useful to drop an additional dimension and suppose (as an illustrative model only) that physical space has one, rather than three, dimensions. The simplest example is where space is a circle which does not change with time. The resulting (static) spacetime has the structure of a (two-dimensional) infinite cylinder with the time direction pointing along the axis.

However, the actual solutions to Einstein's equations are not this simple and, in general, the curvature of space will change in time, leading to a spacetime of the sort shown in Figure 3.1. A special (and very important) example is when the radius increases steadily with time leading to a shape that is something like the surface of an ice-cream cone (Figure 3.2).

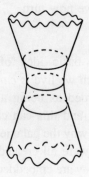

Fig. 3.1 A Spacetime in Which the Curvature of Space Changes With Time

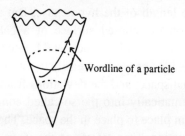

Wordline of a particle

Fig. 3.2 The Spacetime of the Big-bang

This model is much used in cosmology because extrapolating backwards in time we come to a region where the radius of the circle becomes very small and then, at the tip of the cone, vanishes completely. In the four-dimensional analogue of this two-dimensional picture, the circles are replaced by three-dimensional spheres (models of the space in which we actually live) and the tip of the cone (a limiting three-dimensional sphere of zero radius and infinite curvature) is identified with the big-bang.

It is important to emphasise that, as remarked earlier, there exist many solutions to Einstein's equations that exhibit this type of behaviour and, within the framework of the theory itself, there is no way of determining which of these possible histories of the universe is actually realised. On the other hand, a complete creation theory would predict a *single* history (i.e., spacetime). Thus, as with all classical deterministic systems, the most that general relativity can do is to provide a prediction of the state of the universe (that is, its curvature and, if appropriate, matter content)[6] at some time which is conditional on a specification of its *given* state at some earlier time. Looking at Figure 3.2, there is clearly some sense in which space and time begin at the tip of the cone (there is certainly nothing before then!) and so perhaps a natural choice for the reference time would be its value at that point.

It is very difficult to specify such initial conditions since the mathematics becomes singular at this point and any conventional analysis is likely to break down. But even if this was not the case we would still stumble over the same problem we encountered in the case of Newtonian physics. Namely, it seems unlikely that a set of boundary conditions (whose specification would constitute the creation theory) at the initial singularity which is mathematically very simple could lead to the complex universe we see today. Thus, although the introduction of general relativity does give some insight into the sense in which time (and space) might be said to begin, it does not lead to anything like a genuine creation theory.

(3) Time in General Relativity: A key property of general relativity is the position it takes on the general question of the absolute or relational nature of the concepts of space and time. At a first glance, the theory appears to resemble Newtonian physics in granting spacetime a positive ontological standing. Thus spacetime pictures like Figures 3.1-2 have the same status in general relativity as does a picture like Figure 2.1 in the Newtonian world view. However, there is another aspect to the concept of time in general relativity that contrasts with this view and which is of the greatest importance in the construction of quantum theories of creation.

In looking at a diagram like Figure 3.2 it is essential to appreciate that it is the (in this case) cone in *itself* which represents the spacetime - the fact that it has been drawn in a space of one higher dimension has no intrinsic significance. Furthermore, and unlike in Newtonian physics, there is no fundamental choice for the variable that we call time. Although I have shown time as going up the page, this is not to be construed as implying that there is any sort of *universal* time that points in this direction, and least of all one that is related in some way to the higher-dimensional space in which the spacetime cylinder happens to have been

---

6. The equations of general relativity need to be supplemented with additional terms in order to describe the matter found in the universe. These days, one would probably look to a grand unified theory to provide this additional information.

displayed.

So what then is 'time' in general relativity? We seem to be in the peculiar position of knowing what is meant by spacetime but not by 'space' or 'time' considered separately. The key observation is that time must be thought of as an internal property of the system. For example, Figure 3.2 represents a particle moving in a one-dimensional space that is expanding in time. Thus we could say that to specify the configuration of this system at a particular time consists in giving the corresponding radius of the circle, and the position of the particle on that circle, at that time. However, we can avoid reference to this undefined 'time' by specifying instead the position of the particle at each value of the radius of the spatial circle. Or, in other words, we could *define* 'time' to be the radius of the circle. Of course, the statement that the universe is expanding in time then becomes essentially tautological but, as far as the matter content of the universe is concerned, this affords a perfectly workable definition.

In the real situation where space has three (not one)[7] dimensions, an analogous definition of an internal time is the *volume* of the universe. Thus, in this approach, to specify the dynamical evolution of the universe is to say how the components of the metric tensor (and the matter variables) are correlated with the volume of space.

It is important to appreciate that there are many other ways of defining an internal time, none of which has any preferred status. In fact, given a four-dimensional spacetime M, a choice of time is associated with *any* way of slicing M into a collection of three-dimensional spacelike surfaces in which the elements of the collection are labelled by a single real number that increases steadily from one slice to the next (Figure 3.3). All the points on a single slice are simultaneous with each other with respect to the time defined as the value of this labelling parameter. This idea that, rather than being a fixed, external concept, 'time' is an internal property of the system is of considerable significance and plays a central role in quantum theories of creation.

---

7. Some of the more speculative "theories of everything" suggest that, at very small distances, the dimension of space may be bigger than three. However, this does not affect the basic ideas being developed here.

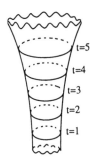

Fig. 3.3 Time as a Slicing of Spacetime

4. *Quantum General Relativity*

(1) *Quantum theory:* The crucial step in the scientific discussion of creation is the introduction of quantum theory into the picture given by general relativity. To illustrate the basic ideas of quantum theory let us consider a simple Newtonian model of a particle moving in a two-dimensional plane with coordinates (x,y). The classical state of the system at a given time is specified by the position of the particle and its velocity; the essential causality of the model is reflected in Newton's equations of motion which lead to a unique state at any later (or earlier) time as a function of this initial data.

The quantum version of this situation is radically different. The state of the system is now specified by a function $\Psi(x, y)$ that gives only the *probability* that the particle will be found at (x, y) if its position is measured.[8] This introduction of probabilistic structure is thought to correspond to an irreducible property of Nature in the sense that, even *in principle*, the theory cannot say what the position of the particle actually *is*; indeed, the concept of the particle 'having' such a position (that is, independently of the measurement process) is very difficult to sustain.[9] These references to measurement and finding the particle

---

8. More precisely, $\Psi(x, y)$ is a complex number and it is $|\Psi(x, y)|^2$ that gives this probability.

9. In classical statistical physics, the use of probability is primarily *epistemological*, that is, it is a measure of our lack of knowledge of the details of the system which,

somewhere (as opposed to the particle *being* somewhere) introduce an instrumentalist/operationalist element into quantum theory that is difficult to remove. This poses a particular problem in the context of quantum cosmology since it is now the state of the entire universe that is being considered and there is no place where an external observer can sit to make his, her, or its measurements! We will return to some of these conceptual issues in the concluding section of the paper.

It is important to emphasise that, notwithstanding the emphasis on probability, dynamical evolution in quantum theory is as causal as it is in classical physics. The only difference is that it is the *probabilities* of finding various configurations that evolve deterministically, rather than the configurations themselves. The mathematical representation of this situation is that (i) the Ψ-function possesses a time label t, and (ii) the change of $\Psi_t(x, y)$ in time is determined by an equation that yields a unique state-function at any time given the value of the state-function at some earlier (or later) time. One consequence of this deterministic picture is that the problem of constructing a creation theory is no easier in the quantum world than it is in the classical one. A complete quantum creation theory would yield, for each time t, a *unique* state-function Ψ_t from which the probabilities of the configurations of all the entities in the universe could be computed. However, all that normal quantum theory gives is the possibility of computing the state function at some given time in terms of the state at any earlier (or later) time. And this is no creation theory at all unless there is some special initial time at which one can give a mathematically simple specification of the quantum state which then evolves into the very complicated state of the observed universe. But, once again, this seems to be ruled out by the notion of the conservation of complexity.

(2) *Quantum gravity:* To escape this impasse we must employ a formalism in which it is no longer appropriate to attach a conventional time label to the quantum states. This entails moving away from the Newtonian (and, indeed, special relativistic) concept of time, and the only known framework in which this can be achieved is that of general relativity. Thus we are lead to contemplate the construction of a creation theory that is based on some combination of quantum theory and general relativity.This will not be easy since, as we have remarked

---

it is assumed, could always be improved by making more accurate measurements. On the other hand, in the conventional interpretation of quantum theory, 'probability' is thought of in a more *ontological* sense as referring to an intrinsic property of reality itself, rather than to our knowledge of it.

already, a complete reconciliation and/or unification of these very disparate conceptual frameworks remains one of the major goals of theoretical physics. However, certain general properties are expected to hold in *any* such theory, and these will suffice for our present purposes.

In the quantum theory of a particle moving in the x-y plane, the state of a system at time t is represented by a function $\Psi_t(x,y)$ which yields the probability of finding the particle at position (x,y) at time t. In a quantum theory of general relativity, the analogous object is expected to be a function Ψ(curv) which tells us the probability of finding a particular three-dimensional space curv if we measure the curvature of space (i.e., the gravitational field) everywhere. If matter is present (in the form of fields or particles) the appropriate function is of the form Ψ(curv,matter) and gives the probability distribution of the matter variables and the curvature of space.

The most important thing to notice about this quantum gravity state function is that it does *not* carry a time label. This is not a typographical error on my part but rather reflects the deep property of general relativity alluded to earlier whereby 'time' is not an external entity but is rather to be regarded as an internal function of the system's variables (such as, for example, the volume of the curved three-space[10]).

At first sight it is not easy to see how any idea of dynamical evolution (and especially creation!) can be extracted from the function Ψ(curv,matter) - since it carries no time label, surely nothing can change in time? This so-called "frozen" formalism caused much confusion when it was first discovered and it took some time for the paradox to be unravelled. But the basic idea is simple enough: one must take seriously the idea of an internal time and use *it* to discuss how the quantum states of the remaining variables evolve. To be more specific, let us choose volume as internal time, and let curv' denote all those curvature variables that remain after removing the volume variable. Then our state function can be written as Ψ(curv',matter,vol) and the crucial idea is to interpret this as the quantum state for the curv' and matter variables at the value vol of the internal time. Alternatively, some of the matter variables could be used to define[11]the passage of time, giving rise to the idea of quantum clocks. In either

---

10.   The phrase 'three-space' is short for 'three-dimensional space'.

11.   I say 'define' rather than 'measure' because, unlike the situation in Newtonian physics, there is no absolute background time to which the matter clock is responding. Thus the position of the hands of a clock does not measure time - it *is* time. Of course, this changes somewhat the meaning of the question of whether or

PEARLMAN MEMORIAL LIBRARY
CENTRAL BIBLE COLLEGE
SPRINGFIELD, MO 65803

case we may say that time is phenomenological and is determined by the contents (gravitational or material) of the universe rather than, as in the case of Newtonian physics, being a fixed, external measure. There are many possible choices for such a'time' and a recurring problem in quantum gravity is to understand if, and how, the results depend on the choice made.

A major technical step is to show that, if they are re-expressed in terms of these new variables, the quantum equations satisfied by the state Ψ(curv,matter) look like standard dynamical evolution equations. This almost works. 'Almost' in the sense that, for the various choices of phenomenological time that have been tested so far, the ensuing equations resemble, but are not exactly the same as, the time evolution equations of conventional quantum theory. But this is just what we want. If the reconstructed evolution equations had been exactly the usual ones, the same rigid causality problem would be encountered and it would not be possible to construct a creation theory. However, the deviation from normality turns out to be precisely what is needed to avoid this causal problem and hence to build a genuine creation theory. Of course, this also entails a subtle change in the meaning ascribed to 'time' around the critical region, and I will explain later what happens within the context of one specific theory.

But we are jumping ahead of ourselves since, even if a phenomenological time can be introduced in this way, we are still far from having a creation theory. Such a theory would yield a *unique* function Ψ(curv,matter) which could be interpreted in the way indicated above to predict: (1) *how much* matter and curvature is present, within the general probabilistic limitations of quantum theory; and (2) what it is *doing* as a function of some phenomenological time. However, the quantum equations satisfied by this function are expected to admit many solutions, and so we are back to the problem we have encountered already in the contexts of Newtonian physics, classical general relativity and conventional quantum theory. To proceed further we must look more carefully at the state-function Ψ(curv,matter) and the ways in which a unique one might be selected.

---

not a particular clock is a good timekeeper!

PEARLMAN MEMORIAL LIBRARY
CENTRAL BIBLE COLLEGE
SPRINGFIELD, MO. 65802

5. *Quantum Theories of Creation*

There are several ways in which one might address the key problem of how to select one particular solution from the plethora of possible probabilistic distributions for the universe. One well-known example is the work of Hartle and Hawking[12] but, since I have written about this elsewhere,[13] I will concentrate here on Vilenkin's method which is also representative of several other schemes.

(1) *Superspace:* A key concept in quantum gravity is *superspace*, defined to be the mathematical space S of all curved, three-dimensional spaces. If matter is present, the definition of superspace is extended to be the set of all pairs (curv, matter) of curved three-spaces and matter configurations on such spaces. Thus we could say that superspace is the space of all *possible* universes, where 'possible' means within the framework of a specific choice for the extension of general relativity to include matter.

Superspace is important because it is the domain space of the quantum gravity state function Ψ; that is, Ψ assigns a complex number Ψ(curv, matter) to each point (curv, matter) in S. The mathematical space S is very large (it has an infinite dimension) and it is difficult to picture. However, it plays a central role in the construction of creation theories.

It is particularly important to understand what a classical spacetime looks like in this context. To this end, consider a path in S that joins together the points $(\text{curv}_1, \text{matter}_1)$ and $(\text{curv}_2, \text{matter}_2)$ where matter_1 and matter_2 are configurations of matter variables on the curved three-spaces curv_1 and curv_2 respectively. Each point on the path represents a matter configuration on a particular curved three-space, and the entire family of such points corresponds to a four-dimensional spacetime (plus matter) that has the three-spaces curv_1 and curv_2 as a pair of boundaries. Thus the path corresponds to a preferred slicing of this spacetime with each point on the path representing the corresponding slice (Figure 5.1).

12. J.B. Hartle and S.W. Hawking, "Wave function of the universe", *Physical Review* D28 (1983), 2960.

13. Isham, "Creation of the universe".

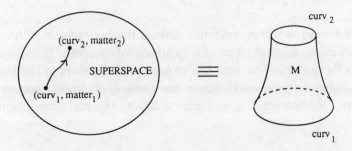

Fig. 5.1 A Curve in Superspace Corresponds to a Four-Dimensional Spacetime Plus Matter.

Any parametrisation of the path provides an admissible measure of time on the spacetime provided only that the parameter value increases steadily along the path; in this sense, we could say that each path is a possible *history* of the universe. Conversely, given a four-dimensional spacetime with a pair of boundaries $curv_1$ and $curv_2$ (on which the matter variables have values $matter_1$ and $matter_2$), choose any way of slicing it into a one-parameter family of spacelike three-surfaces (plus a matter configuration on each slice) such that the two end slices are $curv_1$ and $curv_2$ and with the matter values $matter_1$ and $matter_2$ respectively.Then this one-parameter family defines a path in S that joins together the points $(curv_1, matter_1)$ and $(curv_2, matter_2)$. But note that this slicing can be performed in many different ways (corresponding to the many different choices of phenomenological time), and each generates a different path in S. Thus a more accurate statement is that a four-dimensional spacetime plus matter corresponds to a bundle of paths in S each of which joins together the two points representing the boundary three-spaces and their matter configurations.

To arrive at the quantum mechanical analogue of the above one might consider first a state-function Ψ which vanishes except on those curved three-spaces that are some spacelike slice of a particular four-dimensional spacetime M. Then the probability of finding a three-space is zero unless it is such a slice, and in this sense Ψ could be said to be associated with the classical spacetime M. In practice, the equations of quantum gravity are such that a typical state-function of this type is non-vanishing on a set of three-spaces that is *larger* than the set of spacelike slices of any one four-space. The most that can be hoped for is that Ψ is sharply peaked around such a set, thus giving an *approximate* spacetime picture.

Although this picture is fairly easy to understand it does not in fact correspond to the type of state function that is produced by a typical QCU theory. Instead, such a state oscillates rapidly in certain directions in superspace in such a way as to lead to a high quantum-mechanical correlation between the curvature and matter variables and their velocities. In turn, these correlations generate a whole *set* of classical histories for the universe and its constituents. Thus, not only is the spacetime picture afforded by the quantum theory an approximate one, it is also not unique since the single state function Ψ is associated with more than one classical spacetime.

(2) *The Vilenkin scheme:* A key role is played in creation theories by the natural *boundary* of superspace S. A point in the boundary is associated with a sequence of points in S (i.e., a sequence of possible universes) that appears to converge to something which does not itself belong to S.

A boundary point represents a configuration of the universe that is singular in some way. Examples are when an infinite value is possessed by the curvature or volume of the three-space, or by one or more of the matter variables in the theory. Some of these points correspond to situations in which *spacetime* is also singular (for example, the tip of the cone in Figure 3.2) and are said to belong to the *singular* part of the boundary. Thus a curve in S which represents a classical universe starting with a big-bang would emerge from this singular boundary (see Figure 5.2).

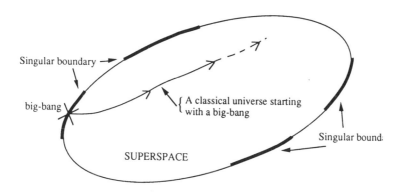

Fig. 5.2 The Boundary of Superspace

The key idea is to try to select a unique function Ψ by specifying its behaviour in some natural and/or simple way on the boundary of superspace. Such a procedure rests on the hope that, at any (phenomenological) time, the configuration of the actual universe (which is very complicated) can be predicted (in a quantum mechanical sense) in terms of boundary conditions on S that are very *simple*. As emphasised earlier, the analogous procedure in classical general relativity (specifying a unique history of the universe in terms of the limit of its configurations as one goes towards the initial big-bang singularity) would not be expected to work because of the presumed conservation of complexity as the system evolves in time.

An important example of such a QCU theory is that due to Vilenkin[14] who suggested that a particular solution Ψ to the quantum gravity equations should be selected by requiring that, at the singular boundary, the flux associated with Ψ always points out of superspace. The idea of a 'flux' can be given a precise mathematical definition but the following rough idea will suffice for our purposes. First, suppose the function Ψ is such that it has the oscillatory behaviour mentioned earlier that is associated with a family of classical solutions to the Einstein equations. In particular, this guarantees that the world which finally emerges from the originating quantum regime is classical - an important requirement for any creation theory that is to agree with our actual universe.

If this condition is satisfied, Vilenkin's boundary condition is essentially that, at the singular boundary of S, the paths in S corresponding to the classical spacetimes associated with Ψ should all be so oriented that they appear to be moving out of S. This allows classical spacetimes that end at a spacetime singularity, or which expand for ever (so that the three-slices tend to a three-space with infinite volume) but, for example, it excludes an expanding universe that *begins* at a spacetime singularity.

The crucial question is the extent to which this scheme generates a genuine creation theory. We recall that there are two aspects to this. The first is whether the scheme yields a *description* of the origination event, and the second is whether it yields a *unique* quantum state Ψ. If the latter is false, the best to be hoped for vis-a-vis the former is that the various quantum states which satisfy the Vilenkin condition all lead to the same general picture of the origination event.

Various approximate calculations have been performed that do indeed predict a unique state function Ψ. However, these approximations involve

---

14. Summarised in A. Vilenkin, "Quantum cosmology and the initial state of the universe", in *Physical Review* D37 (1988), 888.

ignoring all but a small number of the infinite degrees of freedom of the universe that are contained in S and it is by no means clear that the uniqueness will be preserved in the full theory.

(3) *Where does the universe come from?:* The situation in regard to the more modest goal of producing a *description* of the origination event/region is a little more promising and an, at least plausible, answer can be given to the question of what is meant by the beginning of time. A crucial role is played by the observation that the classical spacetimes associated with the state function Ψ have the property that Ψ oscillates rapidly along the path in S corresponding to the spacetime. However, there are regions in S (that depend on Ψ and the precise choice of matter and its interactions) in which no such oscillatory behaviour is possible and that cannot therefore correspond in any way to a classical spacetime.

Thus there is an internal boundary in superspace that separates the regions in which Ψ oscillates - where there is some sort of underlying classical picture - from those where there are no such oscillations and which are therefore purely quantum-mechanical. This is illustrated in Figure 5.3 which also shows the paths corresponding to the classical universes that we are presuming to be associated with the wave function Ψ.

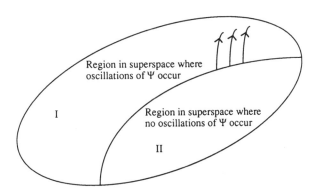

Fig. 5.3 The Boundary in Superspace That Separates the Region Where Oscillations of Ψ Occur From Those Where There Are No Such Oscillations.

A path in the region (I) of superspace where oscillations occur, corresponds to a genuine spacetime (plus matter) - typically a standard, expanding, universe except that it starts (at the internal boundary) with a finite radius, not with the zero radius of the big-bang. However, and this is the crucial point, the wavefunction Ψ "leaks" into the region (II) where it has a strictly non-oscillatory behaviour.[15] Although this region is purely quantum-mechanical, one can nevertheless ask whether it corresponds to anything geometrical. The answer is that there is a sense in which the wave-function in region II can be associated with a spacetime in which time is a purely *imaginary* number (in the sense of complex numbers, not in the sense of non-existing!). The precise meaning of imaginary time is that the time and space dimensions are indistinguishable, in sharp contrast to the situation in normal general relativity. A typical exact solution of Einstein's equations of this type is a four-dimensional sphere, in contrast to the cone of real-time general relativity.

The net effect is that, just as the state function Ψ approximately corresponds to a genuine spacetime(s) in region I, so there is a sense in which it also describes an imaginary-time spacetime in region II which (very roughly) can be thought of as being joined to the region I spacetime at the point in superspace where the path meets the internal boundary. Thus the final picture of the origination of the universe is of an imaginary-time spacetime (that is totally non-classical) from which the real-time (and classical) universe emerges with some finite radius that is determined by the parameters in the equation describing the material content of the universe. This process is sketched in Figure 5.5.

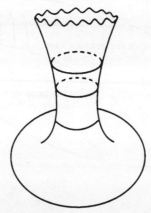

Fig. 5.4 The Real-time Universe "Emerges" From a Primordial Imaginary-time Four-dimensional Sphere.

---

15. This is similar to the quantum tunnelling phenomenon that plays an important role in many practical applications of conventional quantum mechanics.

Of course, the words 'emerge' and 'process' must be understood in a symbolic sense since their usual temporal implications are not appropriate in the present situation: time as we normally understand the word is only applicable in the region of Figure 5.4 that is well away from the originating four-sphere, and then of course it is a phenomenological time in the sense we have described already, not a fundamental time of the type envisaged by Newton. It is important to emphasise that there are *no* real-time solutions to Einstein's equations of the form in Figure 5.4. The nearest one can get is the cone-like spacetime depicted in Figure 3.2. And of course, unlike the four-space in Figure 5.4, this has an initial singularity.

(4) *Other creation schemes:* Several other schemes have been suggested for selecting a unique quantum state from among the possible solutions to the equations of quantum gravity. Although these schemes differ in their details they all agree on the idea that space and time emerge in some way from a purely quantum-mechanical region that can be described in some respects as if it were a classical, imaginary-time four-space. In particular, the Hartle-Hawking picture of creation is very similar to that of Figure 5.4.

Another possibility with imaginary time is multiple universe production. This is sketched in Figure 5.5 which shows an imaginary-time four-space from which emerges a pair of universes in each of which a phenomenological (real) time must be employed. Of course, there is nothing special about the number two, and schemes of this type predict the production of an arbitrary (but finite) number of universes.

Note that, unlike the creation in a *fixed* spacetime discussed in section II, a production of multiple universes does not necessarily mean that the individual universes will interfere with each other. This is because space and time are themselves created, not just the material content of the universe. This explains why I use the phrase multiple universes rather than referring to a single universe defined to be all that there is. In fact, one does not talk about the universe as being all that there is, rather one means all that there is at a given *time*. But there is no distinguished way of correlating the phenomenological times in the two branches of the universe in Figure 5.5, and hence the justification for employing the adjective 'multiple'.

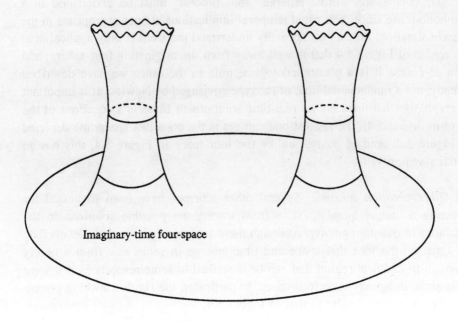

Fig. 5.5 Multiple Universe Production

6. *Conclusions*

We have discussed one approach to constructing a creation theory which involves the imposition of certain conditions on the boundary of the superspace of all possible universes. If successful, such a theory would meet the requirements discussed in the introduction of how much and what it is doing, subject only to the intrinsic (probabilistic) nature of all quantum mechanical predictions. Furthermore, the scheme provides a description of the origination event in which, what we now call, 'space' and 'time' emerge from a four-dimensional spacelike region (i.e., imaginary time). A key role in understanding these ideas is played by the concept of a phenomenological time which is defined using the curvature (gravitational field) or matter variables of the theory.

Unfortunately, many problems arise in the course of this construction and it is important to be clear what they are, especially if grandiose philosophical and/or theological conclusions are going to be drawn from the world view afforded by quantum cosmology. These difficulties come in various categories: some are internal to the quantum creation theories themselves; others are general conceptual problems that afflict all quantum theories of cosmology.

(1) *Technical problems with QCU theories:* I will list first some of the technical problems that are characteristic of all current QCU theories.

1. QCU schemes are grafted onto what is, in fact, a non-existing theory. In particular, they presuppose that general relativity can be quantised in the way we have described. But the feasibilty of this is very unclear and the most to be hoped for is that any proper theory of quantum gravity will reduce in some appropriate limit to the heuristic one sketched above. Thus the current set of QCU theories are likely to give only an approximate picture, particularly at scales of the Planck length or time.

2. The existing QCU theories all assume that a unification of general relativity and quantum theory can be achieved without invoking radical conceptual changes in either. But a number of workers in quantum gravity (including the author) feel strongly that, in the region of the Planck length, a profound shift is needed in our concepts of space, time and matter. Thus the present pictures of the origination event could be extremely misleading.

3. For any of the extant QCU theories, the evidence in support of the thesis that a *unique* state function Ψ is predicted is rather weak. Vilenkin's scheme gives a unique answer in certain simple models but it is not clear if this result would carry across to the full theory, even if it could be defined properly.

4. The different QCU theories are not equivalent to each other, and each author understandably claims that his or her particular scheme is the natural one. Currently, there is no strong reason for preferring any one over the others. In particular, it has not so far been possible to refute any of these theories using genuine observational evidence. This is mainly because of the great difficulty experienced in going beyond very simple calculations that are too approximate to be of any real physical use - a problem that is compounded by the non-existence of a proper quantum gravity theory to which these calculations could anyway be regarded as genuine approximations. Thus it would be difficult to over-emphasise how *extremely* speculative these schemes are.

5. In the present QCU theories there is no way of relating the *type* of matter present to the origination event. This may or may not be a deficiency.

6. The idea that the universe emerged from a primordial, spatial four-sphere is truly mythical and would have delighted all idealists from Plato to Jung.[16]

---

16. Wagner would have appreciated the notion too: the womb-like, archetypal four-sphere resembles the bottom of the Rhine before the Rhinegold was stolen. For a Jungian exposition of this opaque remark see R.Donnington, *Wagner's Ring and its*

However, one must be careful not to take too literally spacetime pictures like Figures 5.4-5.5, especially near the origination or bifurcation regions. The theories of QCU are genuine quantum theories that predict a *probabilistic* distribution of curvature and matter variables. The classical spacetimes in these diagrams are only an approximate way of understanding the content of the wave function Ψ, and the regions where something funny seems to happen to space and time tend to be especially quantum mechanical.

7. However, just as the concept of 'time' is only an approximate one so also it seems likely that the use of probabilistic ideas is only approximately true. In particular, there is no guarantee that, in the deep quantum regime of the origination event, the probabilities ascribed by the theory add up to one. There are general conceptual problems associated with the use of probability in quantum cosmology (see below) but a set of probabilities that do not sum to one seems also to be logically inconsistent. It is almost as if quantum theory itself does not apply in the region which is supposed to be especially quantum mechanical - a somewhat paradoxical situation!

8. Even if there is a classical spacetime picture as in Figures 5.4-5.5, it should not be forgotten that a typical QCU wave function oscillates in such a way as to correspond to a whole family of classical spacetimes, and the question of how a particular classical world is singled out is one facet of the difficult (and unsolved) conceptual problems discussed below.

(2) *Conceptual problems with QCU theories:* A number of general conceptual issues arise when attempts are made to apply quantum theory to the cosmos as a whole. These are so severe that many professional physicists feel that the entire quantum cosmology programme is fundamentally misguided.

The heart of the problem is that the conventional interpretation of quantum theory is thoroughly instrumentalist in tone with its exclusive references, not to the system itself, but rather to what happens if a *measurement* is made on the system. In the context of cosmology this raises the obvious question: Who is the cosmic observer? Clearly what is needed is an interpretation (or development?) of quantum theory that avoids the sharp subject-object dualism of observer and system, and which therefore has a chance of being applied to the universe in its entirety.

Similarly, the notion of state reduction (which is conventionally associated with certain types of measurement) is an anathema to most people who work in

---

Symbols (London 1987).

quantum cosmology. The meaning of state reduction in normal quantum theory has been much discussed in recent years. One approach to understanding a non-reduced state-function is to say that all the possibilities to which it refers are realised in some genuine ontological sense: the infamous many worlds interpretation. Other solutions involve a change to the technical framework of quantum theory. For example, the idea has been advanced several times that an objective state reduction can be derived from a non-linear version of the theory. Such a change would have dramatic implications for quantum cosmology.

The next serious problem for quantum cosmology is the meaning of the probabilistic language used to express the predictions of quantum theory. For example, if a quantum theory of cosmology predicts that, with probability 0.87, I will be typing this article on December 24,1990, is this to be viewed as a great success for the theory? And what does the 0.87 mean anyway? The statistical (i.e., relative frequency) interpretation of probability (which is the form normally used in physics) says merely that if the experiment is repeated many times, then in 87 per cent of the cases I will indeed be found typing the article. But how is the experiment to be repeated?

Opinions are sharply divided on how a prediction of this type should be interpreted. We are faced here with the old problem of what meaning can be ascribed to a probabilistic statement that is intended to apply to a single event. It might perhaps be possible to employ a subjective interpretation involving a degree of belief but, in practice, the tendency is always towards an understanding based on some implementation of the idea of relative frequencies. In the present context, one school of thought maintains that, in some sense, there really is a large ensemble of universes to which the usual statistical interpretation can apply. Various origins have been suggested for such an ensemble. For example:

1. The universe may continually expand and contract giving rise to an endless series of big-bangs and big-crunches. Each cycle is to be thought of as a member of the statistical ensemble. Hence we get a mythology of an endless return (but not cyclic repetition). This view seems to be incompatible with the spacetime pictures of all existing QCU theories.

2. The initial big-bang may have been such that many parts of the physical universe emerged in a causally disconnected way (although still part of a single, spatially connected universe). The probabilistic statements of quantum cosmology are then deemed to apply to the statistical distributions of properties in the separate regions. Whether or not the universe is in fact of this type is something that should be predictable from the theory. More precisely, we might be able to invoke this interpretation if the QCU predicted that, with probability one, the universe did indeed emerge from the origination region with such a causal

disconnectedness.

3. The physical universe may be spatially *disconnected* and the statistical predictions apply to these separate universes. The multi-universe production picture of Figure 5.5 could perhaps be interpreted in this way.

Another approach is to say that the only predictions that have any real meaning are those which affirm something with probability one. The only time in ordinary quantum theory when it is unequivocably meaningful to say that an individual system *possesses* a value for a quantity is if a measurement of the corresponding observable is guaranteed to yield that value with probability one. However, this is the exception rather than the rule, and to stick to just probability-one statements is to ignore most of the theory. On the other hand, there are some intriguing meta-theorems which purport to prove that if the actual universe is sufficiently complex to admit many physical copies of some system, then one of the probability-one statements is that measurements made on this physical ensemble will reproduce the statistical distributions of conventional quantum physics. This is comforting in its way but it does little to help in understanding the content of quantum theory when applied to the universe as a whole!

4

Potential Tensions between Cosmology and Theology

Willem B.Drees (Amsterdam)

The paper starts with a brief recapitulation of some scientific insights (section 1). I will then discuss the *beginning* and the *explanation of the Universe* (sections 2 and 3). I will come to two other areas where the potential tension between theology and cosmology seems to me to be of more importance though less often considered. Firstly, *time* appears to be a concept of limited significance in contemporary cosmology. This might bear upon our understanding of God's relation to temporality, and hence on views regarding *divine eternity* and *divine activity*. Theological positions developed in the context of the dialogue with an evolutionary understanding of the world may be useless in the context of a dialogue with cosmology (section 4). Secondly, the *platonistic character* of theoretical cosmology has significant potential implications for theology (section 5).

In the preceding paper, Chris Isham pointed out many limitations of contemporary cosmological theories. He thus warns against taking cosmology too seriously. The present paper may seem to neglect that warning. As I see it, it may be a good social custom to plead for modesty with respect to one's own business, and especially so in cosmology. And theologians should pay very serious attention to the limitations of cosmology when they intend to use its results as support for their own position (see, for example, the 'beginning', as discussed in section 2). It is there that they may prone to 'smothering the differences', as warned against by Brümmer in his introductory essay in this volume. However, when theologians and evolutionary theists attempt to do, they may rightly be challenged with regards to the applicability of a concept like 'time' throughout their whole scheme. And playing down the quantum cosmological approach, because our world is one in which breakfast is before lunch, as Brümmer quotes approvingly from G.E. Moore, doesn't do justice to the expansionism which is characteristic of science. Playing down cosmology in order to avoid confrontation seems an unfair and unproductive escapist strategy. I prefer rather to take cosmology serious in order to find out where the issues may be. Like Isham, I have tried to focus on the more general features of such cosmological theories.

Secondly, there is no such thing as *the* doctrine of creation[1]. The issue is rather which doctrine of creation one can take seriously against the background knowledge produced by the sciences. Or, understanding theology more dynamically, how revisionistic one is willing to be.

Thirdly, it seems unnecessarily limited to think of the dialogue between theology and science as one regarding exclusively the locus of creation; it touches on our understanding of God in all its various aspects.

Fourthly, a logical conflict may be avoided by adding appropriate additional hypotheses - as Philip Henry Gosse did in 1857 in his book *Omphalos* when he integrated evolutionary theory with belief in a recent creation by holding that the world has been created with all the evidence of a longer past - Adam with a navel and trees with rings. However, I haven't entered into this line of thought, as it seems to result in *ad hoc* solutions and escapes.

1. *Time and Matter*

What is the universe that we are considering, the ontology suggested by contemporary cosmology? In this section some ideas regarding time and matter will be recapitulated.

---

1. D.A.Knight, "Cosmogony and order in the Hebrew tradition", in R.W. Lovin, F.E. Reynolds (eds.), *Cosmogony and Ethical Order* (Chicago 1985), 151, distinguishes between six different views of creation within Yahwism. "They give voice to the viewpoints and values prevalent in diverse settings: priestly, agrarian, sapiential, prophetic, cultic, apocalyptic". And J.Reuman, "Creatio, continua and nova", in V.Vajta (ed.), *The Gospel as History* (Philadelphia 1975), 96, finds "three or four pictures in ancient Israel, three more after the exile, plus half a dozen or more strata in the New Testament". The diversity within systematic theology is at least as wide as in the Biblical texts to which these authors refer.

1.1. Time

Time without flow in classical cosmology: The language of physics is, at least at the present moment, unable to deal adequately with the notion of a flow of time[2]. In their study of physical reality, physicists eliminate those aspects that make phenomena unique, including the unique 'here' and 'now'. A theory of the flow of time would do precisely the opposite, as it would single out a unique moment of time as the present.

One could compare a universe to a *film* - each single picture representing a three dimensional universe at a certain moment. One can either adopt the perspective of the viewer, who sees all the pictures subsequently in time, and hence sees action, movement, 'evolution', or the perspective of the manufacturer, who handles the whole film as a single entity, for instance in selling or storing it. The film still has a 'story', but there is no movement, no action or 'evolution'. The same holds for books.

In relativity theories space-time as a whole is the fundamental four dimensional entity. The philosopher J.J.C. Smart has consequently argued that all objects should be regarded as four dimensional. "If you want to say that you do not really see a tomato (an object extending into the past and the future) but only an instantaneous 'time-slice' of it, then in consistency you should say that you never see tomatoes but only their facing surfaces. ... if you go one way about the tomato and its back and interior then you should go the same way with the past and the future of the tomato"[3]. Other branches of physics take time as a whole as well. One could think of the formulation of physical theories in phase space, with trajectories representing whole histories, and least action approaches. This holistic treatment of temporal extension need not imply determinism - which seems to be the case in the example of a film[4].

---

2.   See P.Kroes. *Time: Its Structure and Role in Physical Theories* (Dordrecht 1985). Questions about the flow of time have often been mixed up with a linear order relation and with asymmetry between the past direction and the future direction. However: (i) an order relation seems necessary for flow, but isn't sufficient - we do not perceive any flow along the line representing the real numbers, and (ii) time asymmetry is neither sufficient nor necessary for flow.

3.   J.J.C.Smart, *Our Place in the Universe* (Oxford 1989), 20.

4.   One can only sell complete films once they are complete. However, selling is an action in time, and hence leads to the temporal type of description. The timeless approach, without claiming to have the final perspective of one's world at a certain moment of time, need not imply determinism, see W.B. Drees, *Beyond the Big*

Time's ontological status in quantum cosmologies: If a theory deals with space-times or complete histories, there still is time as an order parameter from one side of history, its beginning, to the other side, the end. However, even such a status for time is disputed in quantum cosmologies. In general terms, once space and time become subject of description in terms of quantum physics they lose the property of definite location in space and time. What would a moment in time be if it would not have a definite location in time? Time is a phenomenological construct, and, as Isham explains in his contribution, many 'internal' properties can be used to define different notions of 'time'. One might well see this phenomenological nature of time as a modern day equivalent of Augustine's view of *creatio cum tempore*, time being part of the created order. The loss of status goes even further: time isn't an applicable notion at the most fundamental level, at least in some interesting realms in quantum cosmological descriptions.

The limited significance of evolutionary insights: Arthur Peacocke, in his contribution to this volume, emphasises 'the *dynamic* character of the history of nature'. Evolution, in a general sense, 'can be said to occur cosmologically, inorganically, geologically, biologically, socially and culturally'. This emphasis on the temporal nature of reality at all levels, and as seen from all scientific perspectives, is typical of almost all contributors to the science and religion dialogue. Ian Barbour wrote in his Gifford lectures about the metaphysical implications of contemporary physics: "In relativity, time is inseparable from space. There are no purely spatial relationships, only spatiotemporal ones. All of this is radically different from the Newtonian world of absolute space and time, in which change consisted of the rearrangement of particles that are themselves unchanging. We will find a similar emphasis on change and the emergence of genuine novelty in astronomy and evolutionary biology. The historicity of nature is evident in all the sciences."[5] I agree about the departure from Newtonian absolute space and time. However, that doesn't lead us in cosmology to an all-embracing temporality, but to a much more limited significance of 'time', and hence a more limited significance of processes, historicity and the like. Cosmology is not in line with evolutionary biology as dealing with a dynamic and evolving Universe. Hence, theological insights developed in the dialogue with the evolutionary understanding of the natural world are not directly extendable

---

Bang: Quantum Cosmologies and God (La Salle 1990), 283.

5.   I.G.Barbour, *Religion in an Age of Science* (San Francisco 1990), 123.

to the dialogue with cosmology. That would 'smother the differences', to take up the phrase used by Brümmer in his introductory essay to this volume, not just between theology and science, but between different sciences. Just because these authors claim a universal role for an evolutionary, temporal outlook, they are challenged to explicate how they could deal with the, still speculative, ideas at the frontier of cosmological research, and even the standard theory of space-time (General Relativity), which suggest that the evolutionary presentation is one of limited validity, and not the most fundamental one.

If the temporal perspective is considered to be essential to Christianity, 'the doctrine of creation' conflicts with cosmology. However, in my opinion, it might be possible to accept the cosmological view of time, embedding the common sense temporal view in a wider timeless view *sub specie aeternitatis*, provided a meaningful formulation for human responsibility in relation to human actions (within the space-time framework) may be found. Depending on one's view about the relation between free will and indeterminacy, that might be dependent upon further considerations regarding determinism.

1.2 *Matter and vacuum*

Contemporary cosmology also seems to challenge our common sense ideas about the substantiality of the Universe. As Isham pointed out when considering quantum creation in a fixed spacetime, the Universe might be equivalent to a vacuum[6]. Take, for example, *electric charges*. Negative charges, of electrons, are matched by positive charges, of protons. Thus, atoms are electrically neutral, as is a vacuum. The Earth as a whole seems to be electrically neutral, and so does the observable Universe.

Even if the negative and the positive charges match, there still seems to be a lot of *mass*. The universe is, as far as mass is concerned, far from a vacuum: we encounter stars, planets, and people. However, as far as physics is concerned, mass isn't a fundamental concept; it is one of the positive forms of energy ($E = m.c^2$). The observable Universe contains a huge amount of energy. However, we need to take negative energy into account. It takes fuel to launch a rocket; it has negative energy before. Such binding energy is considered negative. The Earth is gravitationally bound to the Sun: without sufficient energy the rocket will be

---

6. E.P. Tryon, "Is the Universe a Vacuum Fluctuation?" in *Nature* 246 (1973), 396-397; repr. in J.Leslie (ed.), *Physical Cosmology and Philosophy* (London 1990).

unable to leave the Solar system. And the Solar system is gravitationally bound to our Galaxy, the Galaxy to the Local group of galaxies, and so on. Could one launch a rocket, in principle, with so much energy that it escapes all the gravitational forces of the Universe? Calculations suggest that that is impossible: it takes as much energy as the mass of the rocket (and fuel) is worth. Its negative (binding) energy just equals its positive (mass) energy. The total energy may well be zero. Hence, the Universe might well be equivalent to a vacuum, as far as energy is concerned. Similar arguments can be made about other properties: either they may total up to zero or they aren't conserved. The Universe may have arisen 'out of nothing', without a source of material.

The equivalence of the Universe to 'nothing' only holds net. It is like someone borrowing a million guilders and buying shares for that amount. That person would be as wealthy, fiscally speaking, as someone without debts and without properties, but he would be more important to the financial market. Such a strategy also assumes quite a lot: the financial system is taken for granted. Similarly, a Universe with positive and negative energy, with mass and gravitational binding, may be equivalent to a vacuum as far as the conserved quantities go, but it nonetheless assumes that there are such quantities, that it is possible to separate zero charge into + and -.

In the preceding section it was argued that the common sense notion of time isn't applicable to the Universe as a whole. Hence, for a 'creation' theory which includes the origination of time, it isn't clear whether the question as to what caused the Universe is meaningful, if the notion *cause* is understood as bearing temporal connotations. If creation in a fixed space-time is considered, as was the framework for the discussion in this section, the Universe might be equivalent to a vacuum. Does one need a cause for 'nothing'?

2. *In the beginning?*

Two kinds of arguments have been employed quite often to make the big-bang theory support theological positions: 1. the theory would provide the material premise for an argument for the existence of a Creator, and 2. there are significant parallels with the Biblical narrative. We will begin with the cosmological argument, arguing that it neglects the limitations of the scientific theories it claims for support.

2.1. A cosmological argument

A typical example of the cosmological argument which we are considering here runs as follows:
"1.Everything that begins to exist has a cause of its existence.
2.The universe began to exist.
3.Therefore the universe has a cause of its existence".[7]

The first premise "is so intuitively obvious that no one in his right mind *really* believes it to be false".[8] 'Nothing from nothing' understood as the requirement of previous material appears similar to the *conservation laws* in science. Therefore, this rule seems to be supported by scientific evidence for the conservation of energy, momentum, charge and the like. However, those conservation laws that are believed to be valid for the Universe as a whole conserve a total quantity which is zero, as for the total charge (see above, 1.2). Other conservation laws, like conservation of mass and energy, are not applicable to the Universe as a whole or total to zero as well. As far as the scientific conservation laws are concerned, the Universe might come from a 'nothing'. If one objects to this on the basis of *ex nihilo nihil fit*, one is using a metaphysical principle, something like 'conservation of actuality', which is not equivalent with or justified by the scientific conservation laws. 'Nothing from nothing' as a requirement of a preceding cause seems also similar to the *methodological* principle of sufficient reason which seems to be at the heart of science: one should always seek reasons. However, this methodological rule should be distinguished from the *metaphysical* principle of sufficient reason, which states that there must be such reasons, whether we can find them or not[9]. This latter principle is outside science.

The second premise has been defended by Craig through an appeal to the big-bang theory and to thermodynamics. The big-bang theory is claimed to show that there was a 'beginning'. The Steady State theory is observationally ruled out, while the oscillating model is incorrect since our Universe is ever expanding. And the entropy (disorder) of the Universe is increasing, because "by definition the universe is a closed system, since it is all there is"[10]. An eternal universe would have reached its state of maximal entropy. Hence, our Universe must have had

---

7.   W.L. Craig, *The Kalām Cosmological Argument* (London 1979), 63.

8.   Craig, 141.

9.   M.K. Munitz, *The Mystery of Existence* (New York 1974).

10.   Craig, 131.

a beginning. The idea, that a universe at low entropy might be a gigantic fluctuation in a universe in equilibrium, is rejected since the fluctuation would have to be extremely big, and hence improbable.

Both these claims are dubious once quantum theories are taken into account. Firstly, although there were in 1979 nearly no results in quantum cosmology, there was consensus among cosmologists that a complete theory needed a quantum theory of gravity. A philosopher could (and should) have known that there was a limit to the validity of the big-bang theory. In current cosmological research there are various ideas about the period before the standard model, and these different approaches have different implications for the cosmological argument. Some are eternal, others suggest an understanding of time which makes the notion of a beginning problematic.

Secondly, the appeal to the Second Law of Thermodynamics needs a more careful consideration as well. There are three meanings of 'open' involved: (a) open as forever expanding with diminishing density; (b) open as having interaction with an environment; and (c) open as regarding the applicability of the Second Law of Thermodynamics. These meanings are confused when it is claimed that the Second Law is applicable (meaning c) since the Universe is by definition closed (having no environment, meaning b). In an expanding universe, the expansion works as if there is an environment, although there is none. More precisely, the maximal entropy increases in an expanding universe, and this increase goes faster than entropy production during most phases. Thus, the universe does not approach a maximal entropy[11]. Rather, the non-equilibrium becomes more pronounced. Besides, the absence of a clear concept of entropy in relation to gravity makes the application of the concept of entropy to the whole Universe disputable. And the statistical character of the Second Law might allow for the occasional occurrence of states of low entropy in an otherwise eternal universe in equilibrium. In combination with the inflationary scenario the fluctuation does not need to be big, nor is it obvious that a much smaller universe with observers like ourselves would be more probable.

It is thus clear that a cosmological argument for the existence of God which is based on the 'beginning' of the Universe has no support from contemporary cosmology, and certainly not on the basis of the big-bang theory - which has a limited domain of validity. It must be a philosophical argument, without appeal to empirical evidence for a beginning of the Universe or for *ex nihilo nihil fit*.

---

11. S. Frautschi, "Entropy in an expanding Universe", in *Science* 217 (1982), 593-599, esp. 595.

2.2. *Parallels with Genesis 1?*

Cosmogonic legends serve a variety of functions. Besides explaining the actual world with its tragic elements like death and decay, they legitimize social or religious structures and traditions, present an ideal against which actual practices are measured, and provide a background to the ethics of a culture.

In the Bible, the world is seen as created. But it does not present just one view of 'how'. Dominant is the emphasis on 'who', the one God related to Israel. Monotheism is not primarily a philosophical statement. It expresses an existential interest: one God implies that enemies don't have a God as powerful as Israel's God. Important is that the same God who is present in the life and history of Israel is also the One who was at the beginning, and who has the power to create or change whatever is necessary to his people. The world itself is not divine; there is a qualitative difference between God and his creatures. By the way, the concept of 'creature' may well serve to exemplify difficulties that arise when ideas are transferred from one context, the Biblical stories, to another one, our current understanding of the world of living organisms. For example, Labuschagne, in his contribution to this volume, speaks of humans as being created on the same day as 'the rest of living creatures on earth', according to the creation story of Genesis one. The 'living creatures' have been given to humans for food only after the flood. Implicitly, plants seem to be excluded from Labuschagne's category of 'living creatures', and thus from 'inherent (c.q. intrinsic) value of every living creature'. Labuschagne seems to smother the differences, to use again Brümmer's phrase from the introductory essay in this volume, between life as it functions in the context of the Biblical narratives and life as it is understood in the context of contemporary biology or environmental ethics, which certainly include plants among the living beings (even among the breathing ones).

Genesis 1, the well-known story of the creation in seven days, is *not* the major, and certainly not the only, text where reflections on God as the Creator can be found. The first few chapters of Genesis have been overemphasized as *the* story about creation and fall, the sources for cosmogony and anthropology. Such an emphasis neglects the variety of Biblical images concerning creation. Besides, it tends to misinterpret Genesis as if it were an answer to our cosmological questions. From the second verse on, the story of Genesis 1 concentrates on 'the earth' as the context of life. This includes a vision of social life, especially through its emphasis on the Sabbath, the seventh day, which is a major element in the identity of the people of Israel.

Both the big-bang idea and the biblical narratives evoke the image of a sudden appearance of the world. A similarity of such a *general nature* is not very surprising; there are at that level only two possibilities: either the Universe had a sudden beginning or it had not such a beginning. In many cultures there have been narratives expressing such a beginning of the world. Parallels with a more informative content fail upon closer inspection. Claiming more specific parallels seems only possible if the text or idea is taken out of its context. The content is read - in a certain way -, but its function is neglected. Adapting the analysis by Sal Restivo of claims on 'parallels' between physics and Eastern mysticism[12], I suggest the following problems about parallels.

1. Translations: Parallels can only be established if there is something to be compared, namely statements in a common language. These statements are translations, both in the linguistic sense (from Hebrew and from mathematics) and in the cultural sense (a culture of a far past and the scientific, theoretical culture).

2. Representativity: If two statements are used to argue for a parallel between two conceptual structures (say, a scientific and a biblical world view), the question arises whether the statements are representative for the whole. A parallel between Genesis 1 and the big-bang idea would not imply that the big-bang theory confirmed a religion based on the Hebrew Bible, since the most important aspect from the biblical point of view, God's presence throughout history, is missing. Similarly for the scientific perspective, since the big-bang theory describes the evolution of the Universe after 'the first fraction of a second', and not the 'beginning', which is beyond the limits of its applicability.

3. The different functions of language: In science the main function is the communication among scientists about observations, experiments and theories. Conceptual clarity and logical consistency are important for such a purpose. Religious language serves other functions, like reassuring and comforting people and evoking moral attitudes. Whether there is some common aspect of language is to be discussed later, but there is surely much difference in this respect. Claiming parallels without paying attention to the function of language is not satisfactory.

4. The languages of science and religion influence each other. Words used in one context get used - with another meaning - in a different context. Parallels based on the use of the same word might be a consequence of such 'corruption of languages'. Notoriously risky are words like 'energy', 'order', 'nothing', and

---

12. S.Restivo, *The Social Relations of Physics, Mysticism and Mathematics* (Dordrecht 1984).

also 'creation'. The use of the *creatio ex nihilo* formula in articles treating the beginning of the Universe as a quantum event might be of such a nature.

Clearly, the validity of claims concerning parallels between contemporary science and traditional texts is doubtful.

3. *Explaining the universe*

3.1. *Does science explain the universe?*

"The only way of explaining the creation is to show that the creator had absolutely no job at all to do, and so might as well not have existed. We can track down the infinitely lazy creator totally free of any labour of creation, by resolving apparent complexities into simplicities."[13] Is there any need for introducing a creator beyond the Universe? Isn't the Universe fully explained by science? Peter Atkins is an eloquent defender of this latter position. The first half of his argument is reduction to simplicity: elephants and humans arise through an evolutionary process given sufficient time and atoms. Atoms arise given even more simple constituents. Perhaps the ultimate unit to be explained is, as Atkins suggests, only space-time; particles being specific configurations, like knots, of space-time points. The other half of his argument is chance: through chance fluctuations nothingness separates into +1 and -1. With dualities like -1 and +1, time and space come into existence. The +1 and -1 may merge again back into nothingness. By chance a stable configuration may come into existence - say our space-time with three spatial dimensions and one temporal dimension. Atkins idea is based on a notion of 'pregeometry' considered over a decade ago. However, the fundamental issue hasn't changed significantly. For example, Hartle and Hawking wrote in their first article on the 'no-boundary' cosmology that the wavefunction gave "the probability for the universe to appear from Nothing"[14]. I would like to put forward three issues for further discussion.

1.*Testability*: There is a plurality of fundamental research programs in cosmology. Experimental tests and observations may well be insufficient to decide among the stronger contenders. Aesthetic judgements are, at least partly, decisive in opting for a specific scheme. However, what one considers elegant,

---

13. P.W. Atkins, *The Creation* (Oxford 1981), 17.

14. J.B. Hartle & S.W. Hawking, "The Wavefunction of the Universe", in *Physical Review* D 28 (1983), 2961.

another may reject. John Barrow formulates this at the end of his book *The World Within the World* as follows: "Confronted with an emotionally satisfying mathematical scheme which is 'simple' enough to command universal assent, but esoteric enough to admit no means of experimental test and grandiose enough to provoke no new questions then, closeted within our world within the world, we might simply have to believe it. Whereof we cannot speak thereof we must be silent: this is the final sentence of the laws of Nature".

2. *Exhaustiveness*: Consider the following dialogue from Lewis Carroll:
"We actually made a map of the country on the scale of *a mile to the mile!*"

"Have you used it much?", I enquired.

"It has never been spread out, yet," said Mein Herr: "the farmers objected: they said it would cover the whole country and shut out the sunlight! So now we use the country itself, as its own map, and I assure you it does nearly as well."[15]

Could a single and relatively simple complete theory be fair to the complexity of the world? Or, as Mary Hesse suggests, is it the case that for "the explanation of *everything* there must in a sense be a conservation of complexity, in other words a trade-off between the simplicity and unity of the theory, and the multiplicity of interpretations of a few general theoretical concepts into many particular objects, properties and relations"[16]. In the present volume, Isham too raises the question whether simple boundary conditions could lead to the complex universe we see today.

3. *A vacuum isn't nothing*: Though the Universe may be equivalent to a vacuum, as far as conserved quantities go, such a vacuum isn't equivalent to nothing. A common sense example: an empty room still has three dimensions, just as the apparent millionaire only can get started once there is a concept of money, of borrowing, and the like. Zero is still a number, with properties, unlike 'nothingness'. Thus, Atkins account of a universe which wouldn't be in need of further explanation might still need some explanation for its laws. The creation theories described by Isham, which avoid assuming a background space-time, seem to be better off in this respect. However, even such theories feed certain assumptions into the scheme, say about the structure of the Universe being

---

15. Lewis Carroll, *Sylvie and Bruno Concluded*, ch.11, as quoted in this context by J.D. Barrow, *The World Within the World* (Oxford 1988).

16. Mary Hesse, "Physics, Philosophy and Myth", in R.J. Russell, W.R. Stoeger & G.V. Coyne (eds.), *Physics, Philosophy and Theology* (Vatican City 1988), 197.

mathematical and describable in a quantum formalism. To summarize, science does explain a lot, but it doesn't offer a full explanation for the Universe. Science seems to remain unable to explain the existence of something with properties, rather than a complete nothing. And it also seems unable to explain the lawfulness of the Universe, or similar assumptions fed into the scientific theories.

3.2. Religious explanations of the universe

Accepting that the scientific explanation covers an enormous amount of data, could the remainder, perhaps the existence and the laws of the vacuum, be in need of a religious explanation, or at least support the plausibility of such a view? Richard Swinburne argues that if the most fundamental law and its effectiveness is scientifically inexplicable, one has to face two possibilities: either the law is completely inexplicable or it has an explanation of another kind. Swinburne makes the distinction between causal and personal explanations. A personal explanation should take its startingpoint from a person with intentions and certain capacities. These together determine the basic acts open to that person, say raising one's hand. According to Swinburne a personal explanation cannot be reduced to a causal explanation. Even though physical concepts (such as muscle strength) are relevant to one's capacities and brainstates are linked to intentions, the correlations aren't logically necessary.

Using this notion of 'personal explanation' the fundamental law of the Universe might have such a personal explanation: that is the way God intended it to be. "The choice is between the universe as stopping-point and God as stopping-point"[17]. According to Swinburne, a universe is much more complex than God. The supposition that there is a God is an extremely simple supposition. A God of infinite power, knowledge, and freedom is the simplest kind of person which there could be, since the idea has no limitations in need of explanation. The Universe, on the other hand, has a complexity, particularity, and finitude "which cries out for explanation"[18]. Hence, the religious option is to be preferred over its alternative.

There is no explicit use of science in this argument. It might be rational and valid, but that is to be debated at the level of philosophical reasoning without

---

17. R.Swinburne, *The Existence of God* (Oxford 1979), 127.
18. Swinburne, 130.

support from science[19]. However, if the choice between accepting the Universe as a brute fact or as needing an explanation of a different kind is justified by comparing the simplicity of the two hypotheses (as Swinburne does), it is a matter of the utmost importance to understand how complex or simple the two alternatives are. Many cosmologists believe that their theories are of an impressive simplicity and elegance in structure and assumptions, even if the mathematics is difficult. Whether this makes it more or less reasonable to regard the Universe as a 'creation' is not clear (why could one not believe that God made a universe with a simple structure?), but it does undermine Swinburne's argument based on simplicity. The notion of 'basic acts', without causal or physical mediation, seems at odds with our experience of persons, who are actually always embodied. Some theologians have thus introduced embodiment into the concept of God[20]; we will return to spatiality below (4.2).

Swinburne's argument based on simplicity fails. The more general idea of using a person as explanation for the Universe isn't helpful: it introduces the problematic concept of a non-embodied person and leads to the next question: If the personal God explains the Universe, who or what explains that person? According to our experience, a person is also an entity that can either be or not be. That seems to be the advantage of the emphasis on values, to which we will now turn.

Values seem to have something absolute about them. They might therefore be better candidates as stopping-point for questions for further explanations than either causal or personal explanations seem to offer. However, a value lacks effectivity. 'Honesty' may be a value, even though it isn't realized automatically. In general, values don't bring about the corresponding states of affairs. However, the Canadian philosopher John Leslie has recently argued that one might think of creative values[21]. He thereby places himself in a long philosophical tradition which places the Good as the origin of all existence and knowledge. Plato used the analogy of the light of the Sun, which allows for growth (existence) and seeing (knowledge). The Good upon which existence and knowledge are

---

19. For criticisms, see J.L.Mackie, *The Miracle of Theism* (Oxford 1982), 95-101, and J.Hick, *An Interpretation of Religion* (London 1989), 104-109.

20. L.J. van den Brom, *God Alomtegenwoordig* (Kampen 1982), and "God's omnipresent agency" in *Religious Studies* 20 (1984) 637-655, and Grace Jantzen, *God's World, God's Body* (London 1984).

21. J.Leslie, *Value and Existence* (Oxford 1979).

dependent, surpasses all existents in dignity and power[22]. Assuming the axiarchic principle that value tends to come into existence, it may be not too difficult to argue for the necessity of consciousness, and hence for characteristics which our environment happens to have. Holding such a philosophical position, it isn't surprising that Leslie has developed a strong interest in the argument from design in its contemporary form, the anthropic coincidences[23]. Swinburne's position seems more voluntaristic, the emphasis being on the will. Something would be good because God wills it; all existence is due to the will of God. Leslie's position is different. Not the human will is extrapolated to the divine, but the qualitative dimension of the good is seen as absolute: God may will something, if 'will' is an adequate concept at all, because it is good.

The idea that values could be creative is rather speculative. Our experience is different: all too easily the good is neglected. Besides, according to our experiences, values find their expression in human decisions. In his criticism of Leslie's position, J.L.Mackie has thus stressed that the concept of 'creative values' may well be a projection of our desire for things judged to be good in themselves, an objectivisation of human desires and judgements[24]. Do values have a platonic existence of their own, apart from of the things in which they are realized? Or are non-embodied values as problematic as non-embodied persons? I wonder whether such a view does sufficient justice to the vulnerability of the good, the discrepancies between reality and ideal.

Clearly then, religious explanations of the Universe, its existence and laws, seem to need assumptions about non-embodied persons or values which are at least as problematic, qua explanations, as the unexplained existence of the Universe or its laws. In the light of the limitations of scientific and religious explanations of the Universe, it may well be wise to join the physicist Charles Misner's view who formulated his view as follows: "To say that God created the Universe does not explain either God or the Universe, but it keeps our consciousness alive to mysteries of awesome majesty that we might otherwise ignore."[25]

---

22. Plato, *Republic* book VI (nr. 509).

23. J.Leslie, *Universes* (London 1990).

24. For another friendly critic of Leslie's position, see Smart, *Our Place in the Universe*.

25. C.W.Misner, "Cosmology and Theology", in W.Yourgrau, A.D. Breck (eds.), *Cosmology, History and Theology* (New York 1977), 95.

4. God

The limited significance of the notion *time* in contemporary cosmology has consequences for ways God might be understood.

4.1. *Divine acts and the universe*

Underlying the interest in 'the beginning' is the idea that that would be the supreme case of a divine act, bringing something into existence from non-existence, without the use of any mediation, say through human agents. This section introduces some alternatives from contemporary theology, to the emphasis on the initial event as the supreme case of a divine act. First, we will briefly refer to process theologians who argue that there is no beginning nor a *creatio ex nihilo* in the temporal sense, but rather a co-existence of God and the world. We then will consider some philosophers of religion who have defended that the whole Universe should be regarded as a single master-act of God.

Process philosophers and theologians defend a view for which the word *pan-en-theism* has been coined as a middle position between theism (God transcending the world) and pantheism (God totally immanent in the world). According to process theologians, God is not the unchanging and passionless absolute, nor the controlling power. "Process theology rejects the notion of *creatio ex nihilo*, if that means creation out of *absolute* nothingness. That doctrine is part and parcel of the doctrine of God as absolute controller. Process theology affirms instead a doctrine of creation out of chaos"[26]. The Universe is coeternal to God, but there are no enduring things within that Universe, thus preserving God's uniqueness. Process theologians think that only an eternal Universe is compatible with their ideas. They defend an analogy between divine and human activity, both using other entities.

In recent philosophy of religion there have been many substantial discussions of 'divine action'[27]. Some have defended, with the process

---

26. J.B. Cobb & D.R. Griffin, *Process Theology: An Introductory Exposition* (Manchester 1976), 65.

27. G.K. Kaufman, *God the Problem* (Harvard, 1972); H.Kessler, "Der Begriffs des Handeln Gottes: Überlegungen zu einer unverzichtbaren theologischen Kategorie", in *Kommunikation und Solidarität* (Freiburg (Schw.)/Münster 1985); W. Härle, R. Preul (eds.), *Marburger Jahrbuch Theologie I* (Marburg 1987); T.V. Morris (ed.), *The Concept of God* (Oxford 1987), and *Divine and Human Action* (Ithaca 1988);

theologians, the notion of specific acts of God, in time. Others, like Gordon Kaufman and Maurice Wiles, have opted for a more revisionistic position, seeing the whole as a single master-act of God. I will briefly summarize this 'single act' position as it seems most congenial to a cosmological point of view.

According to Kaufman, "activity proceeding from a single agent and ordered toward a single end, no matter how complex, is properly to be regarded as *one act*". Hence, "this whole complicated and intricate teleological movement of all nature and history should be regarded as a single all-encompassing act of God, providing the context and meaning of all that occurs"[28]. Such a concept of God's act avoids the problems which are linked with the interventionistic account of divine acts in nature which would set up the order that recognizable experience has. "God's act is viewed as the source of precisely that overarching order itself"[29]. However, Kaufman insists on temporal order. "It is meaningful to regard the fundamental structures of nature and history as grounded in an *act* (of God), however, only of we are able to see them as developing in time. An act is intrinsically temporal: it is the ordering of a succession of events towards an end. If we could not think of the universe as somehow developing in unidirectional fashion in and through temporal processes, it would be mere poetry to speak of God's act"[30]. Kaufman subsequently claims that modern science, the big-bang theory explicitly included, makes such an understanding of the Universe possible, even though the teleological end isn't well discernable to humans.

The notion of temporality is used at two levels here. The temporality of the 'structures of nature and history', the temporality of the created order, correlates to the question in cosmology whether time is a meaningful notion in a space-time view of the Universe (or in a wavefunction of the Universe). The other issue is whether it is necessary to ascribe temporality to God in creating that entity. Kaufman does so because he ascribes intentions to God. Time does function, for him, both within the Universe, the created order, and beyond it - as a concept applicable to God (acts, intentions) as well. Is such an understanding of time not challenged by the physical view of time, which links time intimately with the whole created order? Would it not be possible to take more distance from the language of 'acts', 'causes' and the like in considering the relation between the

---

T.F. Tracy, *God, Action, and Embodiment* (Grand Rapids 1984); K. Ward, *Divine Action* (London 1990); M. Wiles, *God's Action in the World* (London 1986).

28. Kaufman, 137.

29. Kaufman, 138.

30. Kaufman, 138.

physical Universe and the divine? If the whole of space-time (or the whole wave function of the universe) is understood as a single act of God, the notion of time applied to God (act, intentions) should be explicitly distinguished from the notion of time as it pertains to the created order; could one not drop the notion of time (and causal action) at the meta-level?

4.2. Divine eternity

'God's eternity may be understood in two ways[31]: Either God is everlasting and has an unending duration, or God is timeless and without duration. Many major theologians have defended that God is timeless as well as spaceless. As Augustine has it (*Confessiones*, Book XI, Ch.13):

"Thy years do not come and go; while these years of ours do come and go, in order that they all may come. All Thy years stand together, for they stand still, nor are those going away cut off by those coming, for they do not pass away".

Or, with Anselm of Canterbury (*Proslogium*, Ch. XIX):

"Thou wast not, then, yesterday, nor wilt thou be tomorrow; but yesterday and today and tomorrow thou art; or rather, neither yesterday, nor today nor tomorrow thou art; but simply, thou art, outside all time. For yesterday and today and tomorrow have no existence, except in time; but thou, although nothing exists without thee, nevertheless does not exist in space or time, but all things exist in thee".

Timelessness may be understood with Boethius (*Consolation*):

"Eternity, then, is the complete possession of all at once of illimitable life. ... Therefore, whatever includes and possesses the whole fullness of illimitable life at once and is such that nothing future is absent from it and nothing past has flowed away"

Nelson Pike has analyzed the logical relations of this classical understanding of divine eternity as timelessness with other doctrines, like *immutability*, *omnipresence* and *omniscience*. Timelessness has consequences for the interpretation of those other attributes; consequences which he does not like. Eternity as timelessness is a Platonic influence with hardly any scriptural basis.

---

31. N.Pike, *God and Timelessness* (London 1970), ix.

"What reason is there for thinking that a doctrine of God's timelessness should have a place in a system of Christian theology?"[32]

Within the context of philosophy of religion, explicitly seeking to stand in the Biblical tradition, Paul Helm has opposed Pike in arguing strongly that divine eternity should be understood as timelessness. He understands timelessness not as a separate attribute, but rather as God's way of possessing certain attributes. For God's timelessness "justification can be found in the need to draw a proper distinction between the creator and the creature". Thus, "properties which the creator and his creatures have in common are distinguished by their mode of possession". Though the Biblical narratives speak about God as speaking, etc., etc., the "introduction of timelessness offers a metaphysical underpinning for God's functioning as the biblical God"[33]. A problem concerning the conception of a timeless God might be personality; as Hume has said: "A mind, whose acts and sentiments and ideas are not distinct and successive; one, that is wholly simple, and wholly immutable; is a mind, which has no thought, no reason, no will, no sentiment, no love, no hatred; or in a word, is no mind at all"[34]. As the concept of person or mind may be anthropocentric, it might well be that one might be willing to concede that God is not a person in that sense, though the unattainability and non-manipulability might be reason to use 'person'- rather than 'thing'-language in talking about God.

Returning to the dialogue with cosmology, there are a couple of reasons as to why timelessness might have a place, against Pike's "I see no reason":
(1) Time is part of the created order. This is Augustine's view of *creatio cum tempore*, and seems a reasonable interpretation of most contemporary cosmologies, the phenomenological understanding of time. Hence, it is not meaningful to talk about God as if there was time *before* the creation - God as everlasting. (2) Time isn't even an applicable notion 'at all times'. Hence, if temporality is essential to God, how could God then be conceived of as being related to, or even the creator of, those quantum cosmological realms where time isn't applicable? (3) The presence of a timeless description, where the whole is a unit including all moments, suggests that it is possible to talk about the relation of God to this whole - and not God at one moment to the Universe at that moment, differentiating moments in God. I therefore maintain that it is useful to

---

32. Pike, 189f.

33. P.Helm, *Eternal God* (Oxford 1989), 17, 19, 21. See also Brian Leftow, *Time and Eternity* (Ithaca 1991).

34. Hume, *Dialogues Concerning Natural Religion*, as quoted by Helm, 57.

understand, at least in this context, God's transcendence with respect to space and time as timelessness. This emphasizes God's unity with respect to the world.

That leaves us with, at least, two possibilities. If God is understood as *a being* - more or less the mainline theistic understanding, an assumption shared by Pike and Helm, - there still might be an order, and perhaps even a flow, within God which could be labelled God's time. As my teacher in philosophy of religion, Hubbeling, liked to ask: how could God otherwise enjoy music? If music is not enjoyable when all notes are played at the same moment, God's perfection, also with respect to aesthetic appreciation, requires that God has God's time. Karl Barth seems to have defended a similar distinction between ordinary time and God's time when he understood Jesus as the lord of time and distinguished between an uncreated time which is one of the perfections of the divine being and created time, with its succession of past, present, and future[35]. If this notion of 'God's time' is only metaphorically using the concept of 'time', there will not be a problem with science but one with language: what does it mean to speak about time, then? Why not use another word? If a certain similarity with the physical understanding of time is intended, such a notion of 'God's time' is hard to fit in in the cosmological context once time is thoroughly physicalized - just like one isn't free to add one spatial dimension in contemporary superstring theories, another temporal dimension is problematic as well.

An alternative would be to deny that God should be understood as "*a being* - a single individual possessing negative as well as positive attributes"[36]. God might, perhaps, be understood differently, say as 'being itself', 'the Good', or - as might perhaps be appropriate in the context of the natural sciences - 'Intelligibility'. That would be a way to avoid the difficulties which arise upon attempting to locate God in spatial and temporal terms.

4.3. *Divine transcendence*

As was noted in an earlier remark about divine action and embodiment (3.2), Van den Brom has proposed a model in which God is understood as having additional dimensions over and above the regular physical dimensions. As in the well known story about *Flatland*, the higher dimensional reality encompasses the

35. Karl Barth, *Kirchliche Dogmatik* III/2, par.47.

36. Pike, 1.

reality of lower dimensionality. The higher dimensionality should have at least two additional dimensions in order to avoid dissection by the lower dimensional reality. This model makes it possible to imagine God as intimately close to all events without confining God to physical reality.

Mathematically, additional dimensions can be realized easily. Curvature may be included as well in order to accommodate some aspects of cosmology. Physically, the concept of additional dimensions would have fitted well into the Newtonian cosmology. It has become more problematic in the light of the scientific theories of the twentieth century. The special theory of relativity states that there is an upper limit to velocities, the velocity of light. However, the unity of God's actions can be maintained only if there wouldn't be a finite velocity as the upper-limit to communication. Besides, in order to avoid a differentiation of places in God, a measure of distance shouldn't be possible in God's higher dimensional space.

In the context of contemporary cosmology, the model seems to run into additional difficulties. The dimensionality isn't arbitrary. The requirement that the theory describing the fields (matter, interactions) of the Universe should be finite in all its possible observable outcomes seems to restrict the number of potential theories drastically. The consistent theories turn out to require specific dimensionalities - a theory of nine dimensions is essentially different from one of ten dimensions; whereas the first may be inconsistent, the latter may be a live option today. Hence, within the context of physical cosmology it is much harder to render intelligible the concept of additional dimensions than in the context of more traditional views of space and time, such as the Newtonian view.

Transcendence in a space-time sense, either as *before, after, aside,* or *above* seems hard to sustain in the context of contemporary cosmology. Hence, it may be worthwhile to develop an alternative interpretation of transcendence, which might be more like the transcendence of the laws of nature, or, if one accepts the notion of objective values, like the transcendence of values over facts. Sutherland gives good reasons why such a notion of transcendence might be important even if it isn't taken as localizable. As Sutherland argues, the idea of a transcendent point of view, a view *sub specie aeternitatis* can be a notion, which expresses the intention to aim at an understanding of human affairs which goes beyond any limited outlook, whether of an individual, of a community or even of humanity. The idea functions like the transcendental regulative ideas of reason, as directing the understanding towards a certain goal. The unattainability, the transcendence, is essential. It is sane to allow self-questioning in relation to a perspective other than one's own. If this 'other perspective' is accessible, like a list of eternal values, it might result in fanaticism without self-questioning. The idea of the eternal as referring to something transcending even one's most cherished views keeps faith open.[37]

5. Platonistic tendencies in cosmology

5.1. A mathematical universe

In calling cosmology 'platonistic' I do not intend to make an historical claim. The concept is certainly in need of further precision. For the moment I merely intend to draw attention to a number of different features which seem to apply to almost all fundamental scientific cosmologies. A major aspect is the absence of 'time' at the most fundamental level of description. Cosmology seems to deal with a timeless reality, either because it encompasses the whole of space-time or because the notion of time is one of limited applicability with respect to the wavefunction of the Universe.

Reality seems less and less to be described as substantial. We already discussed the possibility that the Universe could be equivalent to a vacuum (in a background space-time). The variety of entities may be traceable to a single abstract field. From the atom as a Solar System in miniature we have moved to abstract formalisms in abstract spaces. Mathematics, since long a valuable tool in science, seems to have become dominant. Reality seems to be mathematical, rather than substantial. This should not be understood as that there is no reality; my impression is that cosmologists tend to be realists about mathematical entities; they have a mode of existence of their own. Mathematical truths aren't invented; they are discovered. However, they are truths of a formal nature; mathematics may be seen as form without content. Could then the content of reality be mathematical?[38]

---

37. S.R. Sutherland, *God, Jesus and Belief: The Legacy of Theism* (Oxford 1984), 110. See also T.Nagel, *The View from Nowhere* (Oxford 1986).

38. In the context of information science similar questions arise. "The theme 'hardware is software' ... proposes that 'software' is not only that we will ever find, but even that in the same sense it is all there actually is underlying the material world of everyday experience." (C.W.Misner, "The immaterial constituents of physical objects" in C.M.Kinnon, A.N.Kholodilin & J.G.Richardson (eds.), *The Impact of Modern Scientific Ideas on Society* (Dordrecht 1981), 133f.) For a recent example of platonism among cosmologists one could read Roger Penrose's *The Emperor's New Mind* (Oxford 1989).

If mathematics is seen as a tool, it may be more or less adequate in describing properties of entities. For example, in stating that an object has a mass of 4.3 kilograms, one means that it has that mass with the required precision, give or take 50 grams. Physical reality is modelled mathematically, but the model is considered to be an approximation. This doesn't hold for all aspects of physical reality; for example, its spatial dimensionality is generally taken to be exactly three. If, on the other hand, reality itself is assumed to be mathematical, one doesn't deal with approximations. It isn't clear in what sense the fundamental symmetry group underlying the particle world could be *approximately* group X - it is group X or it isn't. "One of the most fascinating features of mathematical structures as models of the world is their apparent ability to justify themselves. These structures are so strictly connected with each other that they seem to be necessary and to be in no way open to arbitrary, speculative alterations"[39].

5.2. *Platonistic cosmology and Christian existence*

Rather than being afraid of the apparent self-justificatory nature of mathematics, as if it would mean a revival of the totalitarian tendencies of science, the cosmologist and priest Heller pleads for a more affirmative response: "This type of rationality is an ultimate rationality. In a theological perspective the ultimate rationality is that of God. The fact that it is a mathematical type of rationality is not a new factor in theology. All platonic and neoplatonic philosophies, and all theologies inspired by them, are always inclined to regard the world as a reflection of 'eternal objects' (which might read: of mathematical objects) that dwell on God's mind. The metaphor of 'God thinking the Universe' is well rooted in the history of theology".[40] The platonistic tendencies in cosmology may well be developed into a philosophy which extends the issues from mathematical intelligibility to rationality, and from there into values. (If one wonders whether rationality is a value, consider the emotional resistance to irrationality as being below human dignity.) Another further development of such a platonistic philosophy might extend the discussion on mathematical

---

39. M.Heller, "The experience of limits: new physics and new science", abstract in J.Fennema & I.Paul (eds.), *Science and Religion: One World - Changing Perspectives on Reality* (Dordrecht 1990).

40. Quoted from the paper presented at the *Second European Conference on Science and Religion* (Enschede, March 1988).

intelligibility as to introduce the notion of spirit or mind. "From the theological perspective, there is an intimate relationship between the spirit of rationality and the Christian idea of Logos"[41]. However, defending, or developing, a platonistic theology with reference to cosmology is in danger of 'smothering' essential differences between science and theology, as Brümmer rightly warns in his essay in this volume. Thus, one should be far more cautious with respect to constructive approaches, theology building upon, or being claimed to be in harmony with, science, than with regard to the critical use of science as a basis to question claims made, for example by theologians about the historicity of nature being evident in all the sciences (Barbour, as quoted above).

Is this 'platonism' coming out of cosmology, if correctly diagnosed, a problem for christian theology? As I see it, there may be three different areas of tension, depending on one's position with respect to theology and the relation between theology and science.

As an *epistemological* position the platonism might be at odds with the 'critical realism' defended by many leading authors on science and religion, like Ian Barbour, Arthur Peacocke and John Polkinghorne, as their realism seems to rely heavily on a view of the world as consisting of substantial entities and on seeing scientific knowledge as approximate truth. However, the main targets of the defenders of 'critical realism' seem to be sociological, psychological and idealistic reductions of physical and religious reality to ideas produced by humans; the platonic realism under consideration here doesn't suffer from such a reductionism.

As a *metaphysical* position, the emphasis on the apparently self-justifying, necessary, nature of the mathematical structures, and hence of reality, is at odds with the common emphasis on contingency as a major aspect of the Christian doctrine of creation[42]. There may be two ways out: either there is still some contingency left, for example as a choice between different consistent mathematical schemes, or the contingency under consideration isn't necessary to a proper view of God. The latter may be defendable if one doesn't presuppose a voluntaristic understanding of God as creator, but rather takes it to be that God

---

41. M.Heller, "Scientific rationality and christian logos", in R.J.Russell, W.R. Stoeger & G.V. Coyne (eds.), *Physics, Philosophy and Theology*. See also Heller's *The World and the Word* (Tucson 1986).

42. W.Pannenberg, "The doctrine of creation and modern science", in *Zygon* 23 (1988), 3-21; R.J.Russell, "Contingency in physics and cosmology: a critique of the theology of W. Pannenberg", in *Zygon* 23 (1988), 23-43; T.F.Torrance, *Divine and Contingent Order* (Oxford 1981).

creates according to certain 'internal necessities'[43]. Thus understood, God could not have created something logically contradictory. Rather the fundamental rules of logic reflect God's rationality. Similarly, God could not have created something wicked or ugly, as goodness as well as aesthetic elements are intrinsic to the divine.

The objection which is most important to me, questions this platonism for *moral or existential* reasons rather than for epistemological (critical realism) or metaphysical (contingency) reasons. The platonizing tendencies in cosmology tend to emphasize the unity and coherence of the Universe. Everything fits into an encompassing mathematical structure. In contrast, one might recall Langdon Gilkey's expression of a christian view of existence: "The incoherent and the paradoxical, the intellectually baffling and morally frustrating character of our experience, reflect not merely our lack of systematic thinking but also the real nature of creaturehood, especially 'fallen creaturehood'."[44] A platonizing philosophy of nature might accommodate more easily to a mystical strand in the christian tradition than to the prophetic strand, with its critical stance towards the existing order.

Is this an important conflict between a platonizing interpretation of the Universe and a Christian, existentially shaped, attitude in life? Is this conflict, if real, due to the limitations of such an understanding of the Universe, or even a limitation to any understanding based on the natural sciences with their abstraction from particulars, from the present and from the flow of events in time? Should one, in order to achieve a satisfactory theology, turn to the subject who has developed the platonic understanding of reality, but also acts and interacts - perhaps guided by that vision of a perfect platonic reality but not experiencing it personally? Turning from understanding to acting may be satisfactory from an existentialistic religious point of view. However, is it adequate with respect to contemporary cosmology, with its suggestion that our reality can be interpreted in mathematical terms?

---

43. H.G.Hubbeling, *Principles of the Philosophy of Religion* (Assen 1987), 148.
44. L.Gilkey, *Maker of Heaven and Earth* (Garden City 1959), 37.

5

Evolutionary Research

Christof K. Biebricher (Göttingen)

1. Introduction

I would like to give a brief survey of the state of evolutionary research. As far as possible, I want to avoid evaluation, but I am aware that some scientists working in the field might consider the prospects more optimistically, while others, particularly those less familiar with the discipline, might consider evolutionary research as too speculative. The latter argument has seldom been raised against the well-accepted phylogenetic theory, which shall be briefly discussed later, but sometimes against the discipline engaged in finding possible pathways to the formation of life.

1. What is Life?

What is life? The answer is: we do not know and never shall. But that is certainly not unusual: the essence of life is as inaccessible as the essence of energy, of light or of gravitation. Science, however, does not ask for the essence of phenomena[1] but rather for their properties and relations to other phenomena. Therefore, the correct question must be: What are *criteria* for life? It is certainly

---

1. The aim and limitations of scientific theories have been discussed in chapter 1 by Vincent Brümmer.

quite difficult to list all necessary and sufficient criteria, but we can easily name some necessary conditions[2]:

1) *Metabolism* in which energy is consumed and chemical reactions take place;
2) *Reproduction* in which the living being produces offspring nearly identical to its own appearance;
3) *Mutation* in which reproduction does not produce perfectly identical copies, but minor changes take place.

I listed these criteria, because it can be shown that they suffice for a system that shows Darwinian behaviour in that it is able to adapt to environmental changes. There are molecular systems that fulfil these requirements and indeed show adaptation, but these systems do not live, because more criteria must be met for life. Adaptation by selecting advantageous mutants among a great variety of undirected random mutations is the basis of Darwin's theory.

3. Darwin's Theory

Darwin's theory[3] might be formulated in modern terms as follows: During reproduction, the genotype or information carrier, undergoes mutations or more or less severe, random alterations. The mutations might be expressed dependent on the prevalent environment to show measurable "phenotypic" properties. The phenotypic changes might cause selective advantages or disadvantages to the individuals carrying the mutation, either in the reproduction success or the survival probability, resulting in an enrichment of the type, its depletion or its eradication in the population.

The notion of the 'survival of the fittest' has produced some confusion and has been often labelled as 'Darwinism'. This term is unjustified, since Darwin proposed a new theory, not an ideology. There have been attempts by non-scientists to apply Darwin's ideas to sociology, history or economics. However, the required conditions for Darwinian behaviour are not met in these fields. Darwin's theory can not be blamed for attempts to justify ruthless competition and racist eradication programs[4], and all future attempts in this direction must be unequivocally rejected.

---

2. M. Eigen & R. Winkler-Oswatitsch, *Das Spiel* (München 1975).

3. C. Darwin, *The Origin of Species* (Reprint, New Yorkk, London 1970).

4. B. Müller-Hill, *Tödliche Wissenschaft* (Reinbeck bei Hamburg 1984); S.J. Gould, *The Mismeasure of Man* (New York, London 1981).

In biology, there is no serious doubt that the basic ideas of Darwin are correct. At the molecular level, the evidence for the validity of Darwin's theory is now overwhelming. I am tempted to explain the molecular experiments showing clearly Darwinian behaviour, particularly the many experiments done in my laboratory[5] and those of my colleagues[6], but it would go beyond the scope of this paper.

The title of Darwin's book is 'The origin of species'. Naturally, Darwin had to leave many questions open and we still do not understand fully the details of evolutionary adaptation. Even though the evidence for the close kinship of species is fully convincing[7], it is not known exactly *how* species form. The reasons are clear: the biology of advanced organisms is extremely complex and only fragmentarily understood, and the enormous time spans involved in the development of species can of course not be realized in laboratory studies.

4. The Origin of Life

We know even less about the way in which life was established on earth[8]. For reasons discussed later, most scientists agree that formation of life was a singular event. Some scientists work on exploring the possible conditions on the planet earth around the time period where we think that life began on this planet[9]. Others speculate seriously whether life may have come to the earth from outside. However, the latter proposal merely relocates the stage and changes the scenery without really answering the main question: *Could life have arisen with finite probability by the known laws of chemistry and physics?* There is no agreement in the scientific community on whether it shall ever be possible to unravel all essential aspects of the natural history of the origin of life on Earth. Many

---

5. C.K. Biebricher, "Replication and Evolution of Short-chained RNA Species Replicated by Qß Replicase", in *Cold Spring Harbor Symp. Quant. Biol.* 52, 1987, p.299.

6. M. Eigen, *Stufen zum Leben* (München 1987).

7. E. Mayr, *Systematics and the Origin of Species* (New York 1942, 1982).

8. The arguments presented by Willem B. Drees in Chapter 4 regarding the "beginning" apply not only to the big bang, but also to the origin of life. The corresponding postulate to *Ex nihilo nihil fit* in biology is *Omne vivum de vivo*, in contrast to the mediaeval belief that lower animals may form *de novo*.

9. S.L. Miller & L.E. Orgel, *The Origins of Life on the Earth* (Englewood Cliffs 1974).

famous scientists claim that we shall know some day, while others consider this task to be unsolvable by science for fundamental reasons. Again, this question is of minor importance: for proving that the known laws of chemistry and physics really allow development of life with finite probability, it would suffice to show one possible way, no matter whether this example was realized in the earth's history or whether another route was taken.

How can we be sure that life formed only once? The explosive development of biochemistry and of molecular biology has shown us that, despite the amazing diversity of life, the basic organization of life shows a wonderful unity: the chemical substances of life, the pathways for their synthesis as well as the chemistry of heredity are identical or nearly so in all organisms[10]. Of course that does not *prove* anything, but, since Galilei, science has shed logical proofs in favour to plausibility. Undeniably, the success of science ever since has shown that the latter approach is more suitable for learning something about nature. The former requires a source of knowledge independent of observation, be it divine revelation or an innate understanding of life by man, but most results gained by this approach could not be reconciled with experience obtained by sensory perception.

Thus the way to approach the origin of life is reasoning for plausible pathways followed by experimental testing in order to see whether they can be realized. In recent decades, we have learned much about plausible pathways for the synthesis of biomolecules -- amino acids, nucleoside bases, sugars, fatty acids on the primitive earth -- and an astonishing collection of these biomolecules have been detected in carbonaceous meteorites. Even though much remains to be solved, our knowledge gives us a consistent picture of how the basic constituents of life may have been formed and assembled to primitive macromolecules[11]. Alas, there our knowledge ends. Biological macromolecules organize the chemistry of the cell and are the basis for the encoding and decoding of heredi-tary information. The function of these macromolecules is founded on the accurate folding of the macromolecular chains into defined three-dimensional structures due to intramolecular atomic interactions. The reproducibility of the chain folding requires selection of chain link substances with the correct steric conformation only. Prebiotic synthesis path-ways inevitably lead to mixtures of different conformations from which the correct ones must be selected for

10. J.D. Watson, N.H. Hopkins, J.W. Roberts, J.A. Steitz & A.M. Weiner, *Molecular Biology of the Gene* (Fourth edition, Menlo Park, Calif. 1987).

11. E. Mayr (Ed.), *Evolution* (Heidelberg 1985).

function. For a long time it was hoped that this might be a passing problem until the first functional structures were evolved and, once structures were available, they would take care for the required selection themselves. Unfortunately, this hope has not materialized.

Let me try to illustrate the problem with the most important feature of life, the self-reproduction. The chemical basis is the replication process of nucleic acids where the sequence of a nucleotides in their sequence can be reproduced by selecting the nucleotides for the synthesis of a new chain according to the nucleotides on the template chain. It has been a major achievement of prebiotic chemistry to show that from the chemical synthesis of the nucleotides to the high fidelity replication process every step can be achieved in the test tube under potentially prebiotic conditions, without the enormously complicated machinery performing this task *in vivo*. However, the trial to combine all steps to form a consistent pathway failed miserably. The nucleotide analogues formed during the prebiotic synthesis of nucleotides mess up the later replication process completely: when incorporated into the chain, which happens indiscriminately, they disrupt the required structure and halt the replication process[12].

Such dead ends are common in prebiotic chemistry. However, rather than concluding from these apparently insurmountable difficulties that life could not have been formed, it is the working hypothesis of prebiotic chemists that an important intermediate step in establishing the chemistry of life is missing. Indeed, in many cases this hypothesis did succeed in finding a way around the difficulty.

5. Self-organization of Matter

If prebiotic chemistry requires a good deal of speculative imagination, this applies even more to the endeavour of discovering the ways in which the prebiotic chemistry pathways could have formed the complicated network which allows heredity and selection. Selection requires an expression of the hereditary information resulting in an enhancement of the reproduction success, in most cases to warrant the very survival of the information.

Given the hypothesis that life originated by the natural laws, the most important---and most difficult---step is the one from inanimate matter to life. All

---

12. L.E. Orgel, "Evolution of the Genetic Apparatus: A Review", in *Cold Spring Harbor Symp. Quant. Biol.* 52, 1987, p.9.

the conditions required for life could certainly not originate simultaneously. On the contrary, it is likely that the conditions for Darwinian evolution developed first and paved the way for the self-organization of matter to life. An experimental study of self-organization is virtually impossible, because no record has remained to tell us how primitive life might have been organized; all organisms on the present earth are probably descendants of a hypothetical 'progenote' cell formed about 3.5 billion year ago and have thus undergone an extended optimation process; more primitive systems have been eradicated by the force of selection. The only feasible approach at present, is to build models of development. The task is rather difficult: usually flaws of the model can be found which would prevent survival of a system with the postulated properties. The model must then be modified by inclusion of additional steps which would circumvent the dead end. Tools are the mathematical treatment of model conditions and computer simulations. The study of models is further aided by experiments with the above-mentioned self-replicating and evolving molecules, even though the experimental conditions are certainly not prebiotic[13].

An example may illustrate the approach. One of the greatest difficulties is the balance between mutation and selection. The few physical and chemical molecular processes leading to mutation are well understood; thus good estimates for early biotic mutation rates can be made. On the contrary, since Darwinian fitness is determined by a great variety of factors, many of them unknown, primitive selection can not be predicted. However, it is possible to calculate stability bounds for the possible hereditary information. The result is that the maximal transheritable information chunk at early biotic conditions has been only about one hundredth of a percent of the hereditary information of the most primitive surviving cellular organisms. So far, nobody has been able to propose a primitive coding and decoding machinery with such a limited information. It is obvious that many intermediary and now obsolete steps were necessary to gradually increase the amount of the manageable and transmittable information. The number of scientists working in this discipline is rather small, mainly because it is hard to persuade governments to provide financial support for this kind of research.

---

13. Eigen & Winkler-Oswatitisch; Eigen.

6. Evolutionary Biology and Palaeontology

This is probably the oldest discipline in evolutionary research[14]. Its empirical basis is essentially a quite fragmentary fossil record, which allows comparison of species nearly exclusively for their skeleton anatomies. Unfortunately, present knowledge of developmental biology does not suffice to allow reduction of phenotypic morphology to genotypic alterations. What we know, however, certainly explains the so-called 'missing links' between different species[15]. Gradual genotypic alterations can produce morphological jumps rather than concomitant gradual morphological changes, because morphology is the consequence of a complicated self-regulating cascade of biochemical reactions rather than directly coded. Despite its limitations, the phenomenological edifice of paleontology is impressive.

Difficulties arise, however, if we ask for the selection pressure which led to the development of fundamental anatomic architecture. For instance, it is virtually impossible that a complicated task like developing a flight apparatus can be achieved in one step. One has to find preparatory functions where gradual enlargement of a wing-like structure could produce an evolutionary advantage, e.g. as heat collector or gliding aid. In some examples rudimentary relics of the original function remain and give hints. In other cases, we are completely dependent on imagination and plausibility arguments.

7. Phylogeny

This discipline has its roots in systematic biology, anatomy and paleontology. Anatomical kinship between different species is obvious, and present species as well as extinct species reconstructed from fossil records could be ordered into taxa, families, phyla etc. Systematic biology supplied the first hints to evolution of species and as early as half a century before Darwin evolutionary adaptation of species was an accepted theory. Genera, families, even entire phyla of animals or plants are thought to go back to one ancestor (monophyletic origin) and

---

14. T. Dobzhansky, F.J. Ayala, G.L. Stebbins, & J.W. Valentine, *Evolution* (San Francisco 1977).

15. N. Eldredge, *Unfinished Synthesis: Biological Hierarchies and Modern Evolutionary Thought* (New York, Oxford 1985).

genealogy or phylogenetic trees can be constructed[16]. In most cases reconstruction of the properties of the ancestor is not possible; in only a few cases possible fossil candidates for the ancestor could be named.

An enormous corroboration as well as refinement of the phylogenetic theory is now available by the extensive collection of protein and DNA sequence data. Even though no data are available for extinct species, the sheer evidence of kinship resulting from highly conserved information is overwhelming. Among others, extrapolation of kinships into the past requires the assumption of constant evolution and mutation rates which seem not very plausible. However, instead of giving rise to contradictions, the obtained extrapolations have brought out a surprisingly consistent picture.

Let me close with a general view about the justification of evolutionary research. Only but a few scientific opponents of Darwin's theory have remained. Of the somewhat more frequent critics of the claim about the natural origination of life on earth, none was able to present a fundamental reason, much less a proof, that life could not have been formed with finite probability by the known laws of chemistry and physics. There are, of course, good scientific arguments why sophisticated life forms could not have been formed *de novo* in an isolated warm pond, as Darwin hypothesized once in a letter, but at present no serious scientist supports such a scenario. One has to admit that no-one has been able either to present an entirely consistent and plausible scenario, how life was formed on earth and diversified into species. So, much remains to be done, but many evolutionary steps have been already solved in detail, and the scientists working in the field are looking forward to many new exciting results in the future.

8. *Homo Sapiens and the Evolution*

From the evolutionary point of view, man is a quite normal mammal: anatomical, genetic and, particularly, sequence comparisons of *homo sapiens* with other mammals have not revealed anything unusual about this species[17]. While the brain of *homo sapiens* is unusually large, it does not function neurologically in

---

16. E. Mayr (1942); E. Mayr, *Evolution and the Diversity of Life* (Cambridge, Mass. 1976).

17. Cas J. Labuschagne shows in Chapter 8 that the anthropocentric view of of creation has no biblical basis.

any different way than in other mammals, which suggests an analogous way of thinking[18]. On the other hand, the capacity of *homo sapiens* for communication by oral and written language is unique in nature.

Since the last century, however, *homo sapiens* seems to be an extraordinarily successful species with a high positive selection value. As long the resources permit, the inevitable result of a positive selection value of a species is exponential growth of its population at the expense of other species and a disruption of the ecosystem, which requires vanishing selection values of all species[19]. The negative selection values of other species has already resulted in their effective or imminent extinction. Exponential growth of a population ends when limiting resources prevent a further population increase. The approach to a new stable population size is usually accompanied with damped oscillations of the population size, comprising periods of expanding and shrinking population, the latter due to famine. The positive selection value of the species *homo sapiens* has not been caused by an increase in its fecundity but to a decrease of its mortality. When a new increase of the mortality rates shall be avoided, the last resort to achieve a balanced population size is decreasing the fecundity. Whether the 'wisdom' of *homo sapiens* is capable of population planning to avert a catastrophe, can not be predicted with scientific methods[20].

9. *Creation and the Origin of Life*

Do the studies of evolution and origin of life and their results contradict the doctrine of the creation of heaven and earth by God[21]? I do not think they do, but they nevertheless *disregard* the creation. If the omnipotent god created the world in accordance with his own unfathomable decrees, it would indeed be futile

---

18. The neurobiological and -psychological differences between *Homo sapiens* and other mammals, in particular other primates, are discussedin detail by Malcolm A. Jeeves in Chapter 7.

19. J. Maynard Smith, *Evolutionary Genetics* (Oxford 1989).

20. The ecological crisis caused by the increase of the human population, amplified additionally by the industrial revolution, is discussed by Martin Palmer in Chapter 9.

21. This last section is merely the personal view of the author. A much more thorough discussion of the belief in God the Creator in the light of recent scientific theories and speculations is presented in the following article by Arthur Peacocke.

to search for the origin of life. However, as I pointed out, the study of the origin of life did in fact discover consistent phenomena in accordance with the scientific laws, and the Darwinian claim of an absence of any teleology in the evolution has much evidence in his favour. While these findings do not contradict the creation itself, they appear to rule out certain possibilities of a creation: we have to accept as fact that God did not express his will by talking with a thunderous voice from heaven nor did he leave an unequivocal mark in his creation to prove his own existence to us.

Chance is a fundamental principle underlying such different phenomena in science as the uncertainty principle in physics, the microscopic molecular reactions in chemistry, and Darwin's theory and Mendel's heredity laws in biology, as much as it appears to rule our fate[22]. While chance allows no reliable prediction for a single or a few cases, the statistical laws permit rather precise predictions for a sufficient large number of cases. The notion of chance seems to rule out providence, planning or will; at least this seems to hold if human standards and criteria are applied. Indeed, we can not discern an aim or sense in our presence nor of the existence of any other species. However, the absence of a sense can never be proven, at least not with scientific methods: it would require omniscience.

The Christian faith teaches us to accept the Creator as a loving father, who is not only omniscient and omnipotent, but also has everything---including all the details---in his hands. Luther gave the following explanation of the creation: "I believe that God has created me as well as all creatures and ... cares and still maintains my life..." This was not ignorance: Luther knew enough about human reproduction and genetics and certainly plenty about the unpredictable perils of life as he wrote this explanation to understand the implication of his words. And to the world this faith is certainly much more unbelievable, foolish---and important---as the quibble about when and how the creation of the cosmos began.

---

22.   J. Monod, *Le hasard et la nécessité* (Paris 1970).

6

God as the Creator of the World of Science[1]

Arthur Peacocke (Oxford)

Since I have myself been involved for much of my life in physical biochemistry and molecular biology, I would like first to outline what I have come to regard as those features of the world which the sciences, especially the life sciences, describe that bear, or might or should bear, upon our theological interpretations of that world. Then I will be in a position to consider our concepts of God as the Creator of such a world.

1. Life

(1) *The origin of life.* What the studies we have heard about from Dr Biebricher indicate is, in my view, the inevitability[2] of the appearance of organised, self-replicating systems - the properties of atoms and molecules being what they are - but that what form of organization would be adopted is not

---

1. For a more extended development of the argument in this paper, see the author's *Theology for a Scientific Age* (Oxford 1990). Section 4 of this paper is also included in "Science and God the Creator" in *Evidence of Purpose*, ed. Sir John Templeton (1991).

2. As argued by M.Eigen, "The Self-Organization of matter and the evolution of biological macromolecules", *Naturwissenschaften* 58 (1971), 519.

strictly predictable depending, as it does, on fluctuations. In *retro*spect, the form of molecular organization that is self-reproducing is now intelligible, after nearly four decades of 'molecular biology' and 'biophysics', but in *pro*spect, even with our present knowledge, it would not have been strictly predictable. So there is an openness and flexibility in the development of life even at this critical juncture which has to be reckoned with as a feature of our world.

(2) *Evolution.* The forms of living matter, that is, of living organisms, evolve - as we now know - through those changes in the genetic controlling material (DNA) that issue in changes in the organism that increase the chance of its having surviving progeny. This is, of course, simply neo-Darwinian evolution which may be summed up in two propositions[3]: all organisms, past, present and future, descend from earlier living systems, the first of which arose spontaneously (according to the principles discussed above); and species are derived from one another by natural selection of the best procreators.

The significant point for our present purposes is that the changes in the DNA itself are scattered along the read-out sequences of its immensely long chains in a way that is random with respect to the ultimate effects of these changes on the ability of the organism to have progeny. It is this combination of continuous random changes in the genetically controlling material with the 'accidental' filtering out of changes favourable to the production of progeny that gives to the evolutionary process its apparently opportunistic character and its dependence on actual historical situations which might have been quite otherwise.

There is a sense in which the network of relationships that constitute the evolutionary development and the behaviour pattern of the whole organism is determining what particular DNA sequence is present at the controlling point in its genetic material in the evolved organism. Campbell[4] called this 'downward' or 'top-down' causation insofar as specification of the higher levels of organization is necessary for explaining the lower level, in this case, the sequence in a DNA molecule. Some biologists have stressed furthermore that what happens, evolutionarily speaking, to organisms are consequences of themselves - that is, of their state at any given moment, with all its dependence on historical

---

3.   F. Jacob, *The Logic of Living Systems* (London 1974), 13.

4.   Donald T. Campbell, "'Downward causation' in hierarchically organised systems" in F.F.Ayala & T. Dobzhansky (eds.), *Studies in the Philosophy of Biology: Reduction and Related Problems* (London 1974), 179-86.

accidents - as well as of their genotype and environment[5]. We seem to have here a determination of form through *a flow of information*, rather than through a transmission of energy, where 'information' is conceived of in a broad enough sense to include the input from the environment on which molecular mechanisms are selected.

(3) *The brain, mental events and consciousness.* It is in terms such as these that some neuro-scientists and philosophers have come to speak of the relation between mental events and the physico-chemical changes as neurones which are the triggers of observable actions in living organisms that possess brains sufficiently developed that it is appropriate to attribute to them some kind of consciousness. This view of consciousness as causal, and as an emergent in evolution, has also been espoused by certain neuroscientists, in particular, Roger Sperry.

The point which has to be emphasised in our present context is that this whole state of the brain (or possibly some parts of it in certain instances) acts as a constraint on what happens at the more micro-level of the individual neurones so that what occurs at this lower level is what it is because of the prevailing state of the whole. In other words, there is operative here a top-down causation between the level of the brain state as a whole and that of the individual neurones.

2. *The History of Nature.*

It is important for us to take account of the *dynamic* character of the history of nature, that is, to recognize that the world in all its aspects, as explicated especially by the natural sciences of the last two centuries (that is, since the 'discovery of time' by the eighteenth century pioneers of geology), has come to be seen as always in process, a nexus of evolving forms - some changing rapidly, others over immensely long time scales, but never static. For the 'being' of the world is always also a 'becoming' and there is always a story to be told, especially as matter becomes living and then conscious and, eventually , social too. 'Evolution', in the general sense can be said to occur cosmologically, inorganically, geologically, biologically, socially and culturally. There occurs a continuous, almost kaleidoscopic, recombination of the component units of the

---

5.   R.C.Lewontin, "Gene, organism and environment", in D.S.Bendall (ed.), *Evolution from molecules to men* (Cambridge 1983), 273-85.

universe into an increasing diversity of new forms, which last for a time only to be re-formed out of the same simpler entities into new and more patterns.

Features of and trends in the history of nature which the sciences now bring to our attention include the following.[6] History is a seamless web, a *continuity* which is increasingly *intelligible* as the sciences with more and more success explicate the nature of the transitions between natural forms. The process can be characterized as one of *emergence*, for new forms of matter, and a hierarchy of organization of these forms themselves, appear in the course of time and these new forms have new properties, behaviours and networks of relations which necessitate the development of new epistemologically irreducible concepts in order accurately to describe and refer to them.

The statistical logic is inescapable: *new forms of matter arise only through the dissolution of the old; new life only through death of the old.*

There is always an *increase in* the quantity (entropy) which measures *disorderliness* in natural processes in isolated systems, systems across whose boundaries no matter or energy passes. In open systems, if any systems are non--linear and far from equilibrium, then dissipative structures can arise and new forms of ordering of matter and energy can occur, in fact *will* do so - 'order through fluctuations'. This is the explanation we now have of the anomaly that puzzled nineteenth century scientists of how, in a universe that was increasingly 'disordered', biological *evolution towards increased 'organization'* could occur - the apparent discrepancy between two of that century's most significant scientific discoveries, Darwinian evolution and the Second Law of Thermodynamics[7].

There is often an element of unpredictability about the future states of open systems. That is, there is an *open-endedness* about the course of many natural events. This inherent open-endedness of such natural systems is compounded when they are living. If all were governed by rigid law, a repetitive and uncreative order would prevail: if chance alone ruled, no forms, patterns or organizations would persist long enough for them to have any identity or real

---

6.   A.R.Peacocke, *Science and the Christian Experiment* (London 1971) Chaps. 2-3; idem, *Creation and the World of Science* (Oxford 1979), Chap.2; Holmes Rolston III, *Science and Religion; a critical survey* (New York 1987), Chaps. 2-3.

7.   For a fuller discussion of this, see Arthur Peacocke, *God and the New Biology* (London 1986), Appendix on "Thermodynamics and Life"; and *idem*, "Chance and Law in Irreversible Thermodynamics, Theoretical Biology and Theology", *Philosopy in Science* 4 (1990) 145-180.

existence and the universe could never be a cosmos and susceptible to rational inquiry. It is a combination of the two which makes possible an ordered universe capable of developing within itself new modes of existence[8]. It is *the interplay of chance and law* that *is creative*.

Furthermore, as Karl Popper has put it[9]: "There exist weighted possibilities which are more than *mere possibilities*, but tendencies or propensities to become real: tendencies or propensities to realise themselves". Such propensities, he argues, "are not mere possibilities, but are physical realities". In other words, the dice are thrown in a framework of laws and relations that predispose to certain outcomes - as if the dice were loaded. For example, there is clearly a *propensity for increase in complexity* at the molecular level[10] and as Dr. Biebricher pointed out in his paper, on purely physico-chemical principles, a population of self-copying macromolecules would naturally emerge. So there is clearly a *propensity for life to emerge* ('life' = self-reproducing and self-copying organizations of molecules) - and living organisms themselves, for different but equally intelligible reasons, also display in their evolving history that same propensity for increase in complexity . The increases we observe in complexity and organization (subsumed under 'complexity' from now on) in the natural world are entirely intelligible and not at all mysterious in the sense of requiring some non-naturalistic explanation.

Moreover, the more capable an organism is of recording, analyzing and making predictions from information about its environment, the better chance it will have of surviving in a wide variety of habitats. This sensitivity to, this sentience of, its surroundings inevitably involves an *increase in its ability to experience pain*, which constitutes the necessary biological warning signals of danger and disease. So that it is impossible readily to envisage an *increase of information-processing ability* without an increase in the sensitivity of the signal-detecting system of the organism to its environment. So we can properly speak of a *propensity towards increased sensitivity* and so a *propensity towards consciousness*.

Each increase in sensitivity, and eventually of consciousness, as evolution proceeds inevitably heightens and accentuates awareness both of the beneficent,

---

8. See Peacocke, *Creation and the World of Science*, Chap. 3; David.J.Bartholomew, *God of Chance* (London 1984).

9. Karl Popper, at the World Philosophy Congress in Brighton, August 1988, reported in *The Guardian*, 22 August 1988.

10. I.Prigogine, G.Nicolis and A.Babloyant, *Physics Today* 25 (1972), 23, 38.

life-enhancing and of the inimical, life-diminishing elements in the world in which the organism finds itself. The stakes for joy and pain are, as it were, continuously being raised, and the living organism learns to discriminate between them. So *pain and suffering*, on the one hand, and *consciousness of pleasure and well-being*, on the other, *are emergents* in the world.

3. Persons

The most striking feature of the universe is one that is so obvious that we often overlook it - namely the fact that we are here to ask questions about it at all. That the regular laws of nature acting upon and in the entities of which it consists should have generated the processes which in the course of time culminated in an entity, humanity, which can know the route by which it has arrived on the scene is an astonishing outcome of that highly condensed system of matter-energy enfolded in the tight knot of space-time with which the universe began.

Undoubtedly many of the characteristics of *homo sapiens* which we think are special to us are in fact developments of, extrapolations of, even exaggerations of, features and abilities to be observed in the higher mammals. Evolutionary biology can trace the steps in which a succession of organisms have acquired nervous systems and brains whereby they obtain, store, retrieve, and utilize information about their environments in a way that furthers their survival. The continuities of human beings with their evolutionary predecessors are obvious enough - in anatomy, biochemistry, physiology, for example, and even, and more clearly perceived than formerly, in activities involved in tool-making, exploring the environment and counting. However these last-named 'mental' activities occur only partially in other creatures and the features of *homo sapiens* to which attention has been drawn above in fact represent a genuine discontinuity in the evolutionary process.

In human beings a number of cognitive functions, that are also to be found in animals and that individually make their own contribution to survival, are "integrated into a system of higher order", to use a phrase of Konrad Lorenz[11]. Something new has emerged in humanity which requires autonomous concepts for its description and elaboration. In humanity 'biology' has become 'history' and a new kind of interaction - that of humanity with the rest of the natural order

---

11. Konrad Lorenz, *Behind the Mirror: a search for a natural history of human knowledge* (London, 1977, Engl. trans.), 113.

- arises in which the organism, *homo sapiens*, shapes its own environment, and so its future evolution, by its own choices through utilizing its acquired knowledge and social organization.

Conditions for the emergence of persons: One of the remarkable features of recent reflections, informed by modern astro-physics, particle physics and cosmology, on the relation of humanity to the rest of the universe has been a reversal of the effect of the Copernican Revolution. This appeared to demote humanity by locating it on a planet which was no longer at the centre of the universe and substituting it by the Sun in that privileged location. Subsequently astronomy in the twentieth century accentuated this demotion by relegating the whole solar system to a corner of one among myriads of galaxies. Human life seemed to have only an insignificant role in relation to the vastness of the universe. However in the last two decades we have witnessed amongst scientists an increasingly acute awareness of how finely-tuned the parameters and characteristics of the observed universe are for us as observers to be present at all. Few would now dispute a recent formulation, in its weak form, of what has come to be known as the 'anthropic principle':

> "The observed values of all physical and cosmological quantities are not equally probable but they take on values restricted by the requirement that there exist sites where carbon-based life can evolve and by the requirement that the Universe be old enough for it to have already done so... It [this principle] expresses only the fact that those properties of the Universe we are able to discern are self-selected by the fact that they must be consistent with our evolution and present existence."[12]

It appears that this principle places extremely stringent constraints on the values of many fundamental constants if life is to have anything like the form we know (hence the 'carbon-based' in Barrow and Tipler's formulation) and is to evolve at all in any conceivable universe. Far from our presence in the universe being an inexplicable 'surd', our presence is tightly locked into the universe actually having the properties we now observe it to possess. There are, it can now be confidently affirmed, the closest possible links between many quantitative features of the universe being precisely what they are and the possibility of life, and so of us, being here at all.

---

12. John Barrow and Frank Tipler, *The Anthropic Cosmological Principle* (Oxford 1986), 16.

106

4. *God*

(1) *Continuous Creator.* What the scientific perspective of the world inexorably impresses upon us is a dynamic picture of the world of entities and structures involved in continuous and incessant change and in process without ceasing. The new entities, structures, and processes display genuinely emergent properties that are non-reducible in terms of what preceded them and so constitute new levels of reality (for the critical-realist). Hence new realities come into being, and old ones often pass away, so that God's action as Creator is both past and present - it is continuous. Any notion of God as Creator must now take into account, more than ever before in the history of theology, that God is continuously creating, that God is *semper Creator*. Thus it is that the scientific perspective obliges us to take more seriously and concretely than hitherto in theology the notion of the immanence of God as Creator - that God is the Immanent Creator creating in and through the processes of the natural order.

(2) *Personal Creator of an anthropic universe.* There are good general grounds for believing that God might be 'personal', or 'at least personal'. This belief, indeed experience, is basic and fundamental to the Judeo-Christian religious tradition. From the scientific 'anthropic principle', we can infer that the world does seem to be finely tuned with respect to many physical features in a way conducive to the emergence of living organisms and so of human beings. We can also give reasons why living organisms might develop, through intelligible natural processes, cognitive powers and consciousness as they increased in complexity and flexibility - and how the development of self-consciousness would involve awareness of pain, suffering and death. The presence of humanity in this universe, far from being an unintelligible surd, represents an inherent in--built potentiality of that physical universe in the sense that intelligent, self--conscious life was bound eventually to appear although its *form* was not prescribed by those same fundamental parameters and relationships that made it all possible.

This now well-established 'anthropic' feature of our universe has been interpreted in various and mutually inconsistent ways. For some[13] it renders any talk of a creator God more than ever unnecessary since we would not be likely, would we not, to be able to observe a universe that did *not* have the right

---

13. P.W.Atkins, *The Creation* (Oxford and San Francisco 1981).

conditions for producing us? Others[14] have seen in it a new and more defensible 'argument from design' for the existence of a creator God. The whole debate is philosophically a very subtle and puzzling one[15], depending, as it clearly does on the presuppositions and interpretative framework that one brings to bear on any assessment of the *a priori* probability of all the constants, etc. - all the 'fine tuning' - coming out just to have the values that could lead to life and so to us.

This is the point at which the truly astonishing character of the emergence of personhood can be properly emphasized. For, we may well ask, why did the world, before the emergence of living organisms, and *a fortiori* of humanity, not just go on being an insentient, uncomprehending mechanism - "merely the hurrying of material, endlessly, meaninglessly."[16] The fact is, it didn't and it is indeed highly significant, as John Durant has remarked[17], that with all its impressive knowledge of the physical and biological worlds and of our human physical nature that science can tell us nothing about why we have the experience of subjectivity. Although biology helps us to understand how our cognitive processes help survival and the neuro-sciences are beginning to help us see how our brains might be effective cognitively, this is light-years away from describing the actual experience of cognition, let alone the myriad other facets of subjectively experienced human personhood.There is a huge gap between what mechanism, and even organicism, can predict and any plausible explanation of the presence of persons in the universe eludes science as such. The concept, and so actual instantiation, of personhood is the most intrinsically irreducible of all emerging entities that we know.

It seems, therefore, that the universe has through its own inherent processes - and there is no need to depart from this well-warranted assumption - generated a part of itself which, as persons, introduces a distinctively new kind of causality

14. H.Montefiore, *The Probability of God* (London 1985); John Polkinghorne, *Science and Creation* (London 1988).

15. See, for example, the discussion of J. Leslie, "How to draw conclusions from a fine-tuned universe" in *Physics, Philosophy and Theology: a common quest for understanding* (Vatican City 1988), 297-311; and his recently published *Universes* (London 1989).

16. A.N.Whitehead, *Science and the Modern World,* (New York 1949), 56.

17. John Durant, 1988 Enschede lecture on "Is there a role for theology in an age of secular science?", Second European Conference on Science and Religion. Published in J.Fennema & I.Paul (eds.), *Science and Religion: One World - Changing Perspectives on Reality* (Dordrecht 1990), 161-172.

into itself, namely that of personal agency. This scientific perspective therefore makes more urgent the questions concerning the significance of the emergence of the personal in the form: Does not the very intimacy of our relation to the fundamental features of the physical world, the 'anthropic' features, together with the distinctiveness of personhood, point us in the direction of looking for a 'best explanation' of all-that-is (both non-personal and personal) in terms of some kind of causality that could *include* the personal in its consequences? Since the personal is the highest category of entity we can name in the order of natural beings and since 'God' is the name we give to this 'best explanation',we have good reason for saying that God is (at least) 'personal', or 'supra-personal' and for predicating personal qualities of God as less misleading and more appropriate than impersonal ones - even while recognizing, as always, that such predications must remain ultimately inadequate to that to which they refer, namely, God. It is of the nature of the personal not only to be capable of bearing static predicates, referring to stabler settled characteristics, but also of predicates of a dynamic kind, since the flow of experience is quintessential to being a person.

For our models of God to be personal they must be dynamic as well as static. So it is appropriate to develop our consideration of the creative actions and activity of a personal God also under the heading of 'Divine becoming'.

(3) *Divine becoming.* It is distinctive of free persons that they possess intentions and purposes and act so as to implement them. Hence it becomes proper to ask: can we infer from what is going on in the natural world anything about what might properly be called the 'purposes' of God as personal Creator acting in the created world? That is, can we discern the purposes of this personal God in any ways that are consistent with what we now know of the universe through the sciences? More broadly, is our understanding of God the personal Creator as the 'best explanation' of all-that-is enriched by what science shows us concerning the natural world, including humanity?

(a) *Joy and delight in creation.* The natural world is immensely variegated in its hierarchies of levels of entities, structures and processes, in its 'being'; and abundantly diversifies with a cornucopian fecundity in its 'becoming' in time. We can only conclude that, if there is a personal Creator, then that Creator intended this rich multiformity of entities, structures, and processes in the natural world and, if so, that such a Creator God takes what, in the personal world of human experience, could only be called 'delight' in this multiformity of what he has created. We can only make sense of that, utilising our resources of personal language, if we say that God has joy and delight in continuing creation.

(b) *Ground and source of law ('necessity') and 'chance'.* The interplay between 'chance', at the molecular level of the DNA, and 'law' or 'necessity' at the statistical level of the population of organisms tempted Jacques Monod, in his influential book *Chance and Necessity*, to elevate 'chance' to the level almost of a metaphysical principle whereby the universe might be interpreted. As is well known, he concluded that the 'stupendous edifice of evolution' is, in this sense, rooted in 'pure chance' and that *therefore* all inferences of direction or purpose in the development of the biological world, in particular, and of the universe, in general, must be false. In so arguing, he thereby mounted, in the name of science, one of the strongest and most influential attacks of the century on belief in a creator God.

But there is no reason why the randomness of molecular event in relation to biological consequence has to be given the significant metaphysical status that Monod attributed to it. The involvement of what we call 'chance' at the level of mutation in the DNA does not, of itself, preclude these events from displaying regular trends and manifesting inbuilt propensities at the higher levels of organisms, populations and eco-systems.This role of 'chance', or rather randomness (or 'free experiment') at the micro-level is what one would expect if the universe were so constituted that all the potential forms of organizations of matter (both living and non-living) which it contains might be thoroughly explored.

The investigations of the Brussels school under Ilya Prigogine, and of the Göttingen school under Manfred Eigen, demonstrate that it is the interplay of chance and law that is in fact creative within time, for it is the combination of the two which allows new forms to emerge and evolve - so natural selection appears to be opportunistic.

The principles of natural selection involve the interplay and consequences of random processes (in relation to biological outcome) in the lawlike framework of the rules governing change in biological populations in complex environments. These rules are what they are because of the 'givenness' of the properties of the physical environment and of the already evolved other living organisms with which the organism in question interacts. This givenness, for a theist, can only be regarded as an aspect of the God-endowed features of the world. One might say that the potential of the 'being' of the world is made manifest in the 'becoming' that the operation of chance makes actual. God is the ultimate ground and source of both law ('necessity') and 'chance'.

On this view God acts to create in the world *through* what we call 'chance' operating within the created order, each stage of which constitutes the launching pad for the next. However, the actual course of this unfolding of the hidden potentialities of the world is not a once-for-all pre-determined path, for there are unpredictabilities in the actual systems and processes of the world (micro-events

110

at the 'Heisenberg' level and possibly non-linear dynamical complex systems). There is an open-endedness in the course of the world's 'natural' history. We now have to conceive of God as involved in explorations of the many kinds of unfulfilled potentialities of the universe(s) he[18] has created.

There are, as we saw, inbuilt propensities - a theist would say 'built in by God' - in the natural, creating processes which, as it were, 'load the dice' in favour of life and, once living organisms have appeared, also of increased complexity, awareness, consciousness and sensitivity, with all their consequences. It seems that we now have to take account of (1) this new perspective of God the Creator as acting through chance operating within the constraints of law, that is, of the God-given properties and propensities of the natural world; (2) a renewed emphasis on the immanence of God in the processes of the creative and creating world; and (3) our earlier recognition of the unpredictability of much of what goes on in the world. These lead us to affirm that God the Creator explores in creation.

(c) *Self-limited Omnipotence and Omniscience.* Considerations such as these on the role of 'chance' in creation impel us also to recognize more emphatically than ever before the constraints which God has imposed upon himself in creation and to assert that God has a 'self-limited' omnipotence and omniscience.

The attribution of 'self-limitation' to God with respect to his omnipotence is meant to indicate that God has so made the world that there are certain areas over which he has chosen not to have power. Similarly, the attribution of 'self-limitation' to God in regard to his omniscience is meant to denote that God may also have so made the world that, at any given time, there are certain systems whose future states cannot be known even to him since they are in principle not knowable (for example, those in the 'Heisenberg' range and certain non-linear systems at the macroscopic level). If there is no particular point in time of which it is could truly be said of those systems 'this will be its future state', then it could not be known at any instant, by God or by us, what the future state of such systems will be. God's 'omniscience' has to be construed as God knowing at any time whatever it is possible that he know at that time.

These considerations do not, of course, preclude God from knowing the probabilities of the sequence of events in such systems and so of knowing, and of influencing, the general direction of the history of natural events.

(d) *The vulnerability of God.* The conditions for the emergence of open-endedness in natural systems - and so, in due course, the experience of freedom

---

18. The use of the male pronoun here is not meant to exclude feminine aspects of God.

of the human-brain-in-the-human-body - involve a subtle interweaving of chance and law, with consequences that are often not readily predictable in principle. If God willed the existence of self-conscious intelligent, freely-willing creatures as an end, he must, to be self-consistent, logically be presumed to have willed the means to achieving that end. This divine purpose must be taken to have been an overriding one for it involves as a corollary an element of risk to his purposes whereby he renders himself vulnerable in a way that is only now becoming perceivable by us. This idea that God took a risk in creation is not new but is now, I am suggesting, reinforced and given a wider context by these biological considerations.

(e) *A suffering God.* If God is immanently present in and to natural processes, in particular those that generate conscious and self-conscious life, then we cannot but infer that God suffers in, with and under the creative processes of the world with their costly, open-ended unfolding in time.

There has been an increasing assent to this idea that it is possible, as Paul Fiddes has put it[19]: "To speak consistently of *a God who suffers eminently and yet is still God, and a God who suffers universally and yet is still present uniquely and decisively in the sufferings of Christ*". He points out that among the factors that have promoted the view that God suffers are new assessments of "the meaning of love [especially, the love of God], the implications of the cross of Jesus, the problem of [human] suffering, and the *structure of the world*" (italics added)[20]. It is this last-mentioned - the 'structure of the world' - on which the new perspectives of the sciences bear by showing how the world processes inevitably involve death, pain and suffering if self-conscious sentient creatures are to emerge in a physical universe. An immanent Creator cannot but be regarded as creating through such a process and so as suffering in, with and under it.

It is becoming increasingly apparent that the perspectives of science are providing the stimulus for a re-birth of images in our talk of God. It is indeed necessary for any theology that could justifiably describe itself as exploratory to recognise that it may have to be re-shaped to address convincingly a humanity that now has the dazzling, and sometimes daunting, panorama of the natural sciences unfolding before it - just the kind of exploration to which the sponsors of this series of conferences are devoted.

---

19. Paul S. Fides, *The Creative Suffering of God* (Oxford 1988), 3.
20. Fides, 45 (see also all of chapter 2).

7

The Status of Humanity
in Relation to the Animal Kingdom

Malcolm A. Jeeves (St. Andrews)

In addressing the topic assigned to me by the conference organizers I was asked to talk about the conceptual issues which arise in deciding the cut-off point in distinguishing human from animal. As a scientist I would prefer to frame the issue slightly differently. Our concern is not to decide a cut-off point but to understand how and when in our study of animals we may learn things which widen and deepen our understanding of human beings, and how and when by failing to recognize differences we are in danger of misleading ourselves in our understanding of both humans and animals. Thus whilst this issue, as I have just reframed it is, understandably, an important one in seeking to relate the domains of science and theology, I would wish to stress that it is also, in its own right, an important one to scientists.

The value of some of our research in neuroscience, and in my own specialised field of interest neuropsychology, depends upon making legitimate deductions from experiments on animals in tackling problems of human disease and behaviour. For example, we make extensive use of animal models in seeking to understand the pathology of Parkinson's disease and in devising methods of alleviation. Most recently the work on neural tissue transplants developed on animals has been extended, with limited success, to the human condition. It is crucial then to have as securely based an assessment as possible of the similarities and differences between humans and animals. My plan will be to identify some of the perennial issues, to indicate how views have changed, at times rapidly, over the past thirty years, and to ask if there are any issues here that should concern us as Christians and how we may face them constructively and with an open mind.

1. *Changing views of the similarities and differences between animals and humans*

(a) *Language, learning and other abilities*

In his 1974 Gifford lectures the late Professor W.H. Thorpe[1] listed a number of abilities which, so it had been confidently asserted forty years earlier, animals would never be able to show. His list included the following: animals could not learn, they could not plan ahead, they could not conceptualise, they could not use tools, they have no language, they cannot count, they lack artistic sense and they lack all ethical sense. Today, in the light of the evidence gathered by ethologists and psychologists, it would be very difficult to maintain any item in this list. That was the view that Thorpe himself took in his Gifford lectures.

More recently (1987), writing in *The Oxford Companion to the Mind* Professor Robert Hinde[2] (also at Cambridge) took a rather similar view. He concluded that the main difference between animals and humans lies in the complexity of human language. He believed that animal communication falls so far short of human language that the difference is best seen as one of *quality* rather than *quantity*. He also takes the view that animal models can provide data relevant to human behaviour and experience and that the differences between animals and humans can be usefully exploited.

On the question of whether language is the crucial feature separating humans from animals Thorpe[3] wrote, "Personally I believe it is safe to conclude that if chimpanzees had the necessary equipment in the larynx and pharynx, they could learn to talk, at least as well as children of three years of age and perhaps older". Today, that view would be debated by some but it gives the flavour of the strength of his conviction at that time. He went on to make other strong claims and whilst noting that when used by humans language is propositional, syntactic and expressive of intention, he pointed out that all these features can be found

---

1. W.H. Thorpe, *Animal nature and human nature* (London 1974).

2. R.A. Hinde, "Animal-human comparisons", pp 25-27 in *The Oxford Companion to the Mind* (Oxford 1987).

3. W.H. Thorpe, (*ibid*).

114

separately, and at least to some degree, in the animal kingdom. Even so he concludes that "there comes a point where more creates a difference, *quantity* produces a *qualitative* difference". Thus foreshadowing the point made later by Hinde.

(b) *Brain structure and specialised functions*
A second area of contemporary psychology where the validity of comparisons between animals and humans is important is neuropsychology. In 1984 Professor George Ettlinger wrote a paper[4] entitled "Humans, Apes and Monkeys - the Changing Neuropsychological Viewpoint". He argued that "The majority would ... agree ... that, within the primates brain size (relative to body weight) increased suddenly with the emergence of modern man; that a large mass of brain tissue endowed man with a stepwise superior intelligence; and that language followed from man's superior intelligence". One implication from Ettlinger's presentation is that intellectual capacity increased only slowly within the primates until, at some stage related to the emergence of modern man, a totally new skill - for human language - evolved. And that language in turn allowed man to gain his intellectual preeminence and to devise his technologies and cultures. He further argues that "... in man, language has more than a communicative role - it also organizes the representation of information *within* one individual's mind. It has yet to be shown that language - competent apes can solve any of the kind of cognitive problems more proficiently than can non-trained apes. By contrast, aphasic patients can be shown to be impaired on a variety of cognitive tasks".

One key point that emerged from Ettlinger's review was the enormous change that has taken place within a twenty year period. As such it is an object lesson which illustrates well the mistakes that occurred in the past when, for whatever reasons, people tried to think up differences between animals and humans which they believed would remain unchallenged for all time and which would enable them to make a clear distinction between animals and humans.

(c) *Lessons from the Changing Scene*
In the late 1950s the Nobel Laureate Roger Sperry and his co-workers reported their classic and elegant work on the so-called split-brain preparation. The term

---

4.   G. Ettlinger, "Humans, Apes and Monkeys: The changing neuropsychological viewpoint." *Neuropsychologia* Vol. 22, No. 8, pp 685-696.

split-brain refers to an operation used as a last resort on patients with intractable epilepsy and for whom every other kind of medication had been tried and found ineffective. The forebrain commissures, pathways containing about two hundred million fibres connecting our two cerebral hemispheres, are cut through in this operation, effectively disconnecting the hemispheres. In individuals subjected to this procedure a state of affairs was produced which offered a unique opportunity to study the supposed specialised functions of each cerebral hemisphere *without* interference from the other. It soon became clear that the two cerebral hemispheres do indeed have distinct abilities. As a result, there was a great resurgence of interest in the whole question of hemispheric specialisation of function. Clear functional differences between the two hemispheres in human beings became well established. It was not long before there were those who asserted that here is an obvious instance of where humans differ from animals. Animals they said do not show this asymmetry. In humans the most obvious hemispheric asymmetry is associated with the fact that the majority of people are right-handed. In such people it is clear that normally their left cerebral hemisphere deals with language whereas the right side of the brain deals with visuo-spatial ability.

By 1983, however, the late Norman Geshwind, at that time Professor of Neurology at Harvard, could write, "It is now likely that no animal species, no matter how humble, lacks cerebral dominance". The lesson is clear. If in 1963 you were desperate to maintain the uniqueness of man on the grounds that mankind alone possessed the kind of cerebral dominance most dramatically portrayed in language lateralities then twenty years later you would be confronted with a situation where functional brain asymmetries had been demonstrated in a wide variety of species; birds, rodents, non-human primates to name but a few.

2. *Comparative brain anatomy*

Continuing our review of possible differences between animals and humans we turn to comparative brain anatomy. A topic with a rich and lively history when we recall how in 1858 Richard Owen in his exchanges with Huxley argued for the uniqueness of man on the grounds that "the great-ape does not possess a hippocampus-minor". The best reference work for those wishing to pursue this topic in detail is Dr. Richard Passingham's 1986 book *"The Human Primate"*[5].

---

5.   R. Passingham, *The Human Primate* (Oxford 1982).

116

He begins by saying "anatomically we differ from the apes much more extensively than would have been supposed from the similarity of the DNA and many proteins. The difference in size between the human and the chimpanzee brain is greater than the difference between the brains of the chimpanzee and the shrew". Thus if you are looking for a way of asserting the uniqueness of man, you might grasp at this quotation. But be warned, as you read on in Passingham, the story changes. He raises the question, "What is the distinctiveness of the brain of humans?" and suggests that there are three different ways in which you can consider this. First in terms of size, second in terms of the relative proportions assigned to particular functions in the brain and third whether there are specialized areas in humans not found in other brains.

We shall examine each of these briefly. First, size. At once certain obvious traps become apparent. Whales have much bigger brains than we have, so have elephants. So sheer size isn't a very good ground from which to try and argue the uniqueness of homo sapiens sapiens. Our brain, nevertheless, is three times as large as we could expect for a primate of our build.

Consider for a moment the typical primate. Passingham plots brain-weight against body weight and comes up with a regression line for the non-human primates. Against this line the human brain is 3.1 times as big as expected for a non-human primate of the same weight. On the basis of this, you may therefore say that we are indeed special creatures. The human brain is unique for its overall size when account is taken of the weight of the body. If size alone is important, there are grounds for asserting difference. But, there are other ways of thinking about a typical primate brain.

You may ask, "Is there anything special about the *proportions* of the brain assigned to different functions, such as areas that receive sensory information or control motor output? Regarded in this way, is there anything special about our brains as compared to the typical primate brain?" Looked at this way Passingham concludes, "The human brain seems to fit very nicely the typical primate brain". However, he makes a further important point. To say that differences are predictable - that is predictable from the model of a typical primate brain - is *not* to say that they are unimportant. The question then becomes, is our brain just an expanded brain of another primate, such as a chimpanzee? This returns us to the question of the distinctiveness of the human brain? Is there one and if so what is its nature?

Passingham points out that there are two specializations which are often said to be unique to the human brain. First, cerebral asymmetries and second, the existence of "speech areas" in the neocortex. Two areas of the brain, the cerebellum and the neocortex are largely responsible for associating information that comes from other parts of the brain as a system. These areas in the human are roughly three times the size they should be for a typical primate of our size. The cerebellum is about two and a half times as big as it should be for a brain of human size. On these grounds, Passingham concludes that the gap between man and chimpanzee is probably much greater than we had earlier supposed. Thus specialization does provide something of a clue to a difference between humans and animals.

To sum up. There are four conclusions to be drawn when you study brain structure having in mind the question, "How does the non-human primate differ from the human primate?" First, many of the distinctively human features can be derived simply by following the rules governing the construction of other primates. If you ask, "What is a typical primate brain like?" and you follow these rules, you get the human primate. Second, Passingham thinks that the case for man's uniqueness rests on language, invention, conscience and freewill. For some of these it is difficult to know what sort of evidence you would appeal to in order to establish that a non-human primate did not have them. It is not clear to me what for example constitutes evidence that a monkey does not have free will. Passingham further points out that the account he gives lacks mystery. It attributes the peculiarly human form of mental life to relatively simple changes in the human brain. Finally he says that in his view it is without doubt language which has led to the transformation of society. Rules can be issued by means of it, strategies can be discussed, roles can be laid down, traditions can be passed on.

Clearly for Passingham, the crucial difference is language. For that reason I think we have to reflect a little more on just what we mean when we talk about language. As far as Passingham is concerned, he doesn't simply mean communication because right across the animal phyla there are examples of how animals communicate very subtly and elegantly with one another. It is not simply communication that Passingham has in mind, rather it is that aspect of language which enables us to handle not just symbols - chimps and apes can do that - rather it is our ability to represent words to ourselves; to manipulate internal symbols. It is this aspect of symbolic behaviour conferred by language that he believes is the crucial difference between mankind and non-human primates.

3. *The picture emerging*

What then is the overall picture emerging? From the evidence from comparative psychology, two things stand out. The first concerns language. You will have noticed that in their different ways, Robert Hinde and William Thorpe both identified this as one of the crucial distinguishing features. Hinde regards the difference as one of quality rather than quantity. It is not that the non-human primate does not have some form of language. We know from the work of Premack and others that they are able to use forms of language. It is rather that in man the capacity is so much greater than in animals that it is most meaningfully thought of as qualitatively different. Fooks, however, has argued that the possibility of chimpanzee language challenges the notion of a sharp break between human and animal cognition. Thorpe nevertheless argues there is a point where 'more' creates a difference.

Thorpe, in his Gifford lectures, having reviewed a vast amount of empirical evidence, makes the very strong claim that we are left with a tremendous chasm, intellectual, artistic, technical, linguistic, moral, ethical, scientific and spiritual between ape and man. He adds that we have no clear idea how this gap is bridged. Man is unique in all these aspects and we may never know how this happened. I think I would wish to qualify this slightly and argue for the possibility (depending on interpretation) for some evidence of moral behaviour in the way that chimpanzees look after their young, and conduct their family life. As regards scientific achievements there is clearly a chasm between mankind and all other animals. As regards the spiritual dimension it is true that animals can be made to exhibit superstitious behaviour, as B.F. Skinner did with his pigeons, but that is hardly what we mean by spiritual! We have no grounds for denying this possibility but equally there are no grounds for asserting it.

Turning now to the overall emerging picture from neuropsychology and comparative brain structures, what do we find? First, the neuropsychological discontinuities between man and monkey that seemed so evident in 1963 have in many instances become indistinct by 1983. As I hinted at earlier this line of argument has a long and not very commendable history. Huxley convincingly refuted the claims of the anatomist Richard Owen made in 1858. Owen had said that there were three structures that were unique to the human brain. He was very anxious to have something that would uniquely define the human brain and thus set man apart from the rest of creation. But Huxley was scornful of those, who, as he put it, sought to base man's dignity upon his great toe or to assert that we are lost if an ape has the hippocampus minor. An ape does have such a structure, so presumably on Owen's argument we are lost. I ask the question, "Have we learned this lesson?".

4. *New directions - Machiavellian Intelligence*

Recently my colleagues at St. Andrews, Richard Byrne[6] and Andrew Whiten, have catalogued the potential evolutionary importance of what they call Machiavellian intelligence. This refers to the ability to prevail in a complex society through the judicious application of cleverness, deceit and political acumen. They point out that deception is widespread in the natural world. Much of this however does not justify the attribution of deception of the kind talked about by Byrne and Whiten. Their concern is with tactical deception. This looks at situations which suggest that an animal has the mental flexibility to use "honest" behaviour in such a way that they deceive and mislead another member of their own social group. The evidence is compelling. It remains, however, a topic of lively debate amongst ethologists and psychologists. Humphrey, for example, has said, "In my opinion the word (Machiavellian) gives too much weight to the hostile use of intelligence. One of the functions of intellect in higher primates and humans is to keep the social unit together and make it able successfully to exploit the environment. A lot of intelligence could better be seen as driven by the need for cooperation and compensation". To which, Byrne and Whiten reply that cooperation is itself an excellent Machiavellian strategy - sometimes. The purpose of mentioning this new development here is to illustrate how yet again some of the most seemingly cunningly intellectual capacities of humankind seem to be represented in the natural behaviour of the higher non-human primates. Again this causes neither surprise nor concern to the Christian scientist with an openly peaceable mind. It only becomes contentious if, for whatever reason, a position has been taken (in the absence of empirical evidence either way) that such deviously cunning behaviour calls for intellectual capacities confined to humankind.

5. *A Christian Perspective*

It is salutary to remember that some of the issues raised ninety years ago by Professor A.M. Fairbairn[7] in his *"The Philosophy of the Christian Religion"* (Hodder & Stoughton, London 1902) remain as pressing today as they were then.

---

6.   R.W. Byrne and A. Whiten (Eds.), *Machiavellian intelligence: social expertise and the evolution of intellect in monkeys, apes and humans* (Oxford 1988).

7.   A.M. Fairbairn, *The Philosophy of the Christian Religion* (London, 1902).

He wrote concerning the position of man and his nature "Do the eloquently minimized differences which we find in the structure of man as distinguished from the man-like ape, explain the differences in their histories?" (p.45) And the burden of his argument remains today, namely, that we still, from a purely scientific perspective, are puzzled to understand how such seemingly small differences between man and the non-human primates have given rise to such vastly different outcomes in terms of the achievements of men in art, literature, science, music, religion, technology and so on - the "vast gap" described by Thorpe. A crucial clue is surely provided in Dr. Labuschagne's chapter which focuses our attention away from a purely anthropocentric perspective to the theocentric perspective of scripture.

Nothing is to be gained scientifically or theologically by glossing over real differences between man and animals. By fudging the issue of the implications of the far-reaching *differences* listed above with sentimental slogans which sound compassionate serves the best interests of neither animals nor men. We simply "deceive ourselves and the truth is not in us". At the same time there are no scientific or theological issues at stake by fully recognizing the many and equally important *similarities* between men and animals - a point emphasized and given its scriptural basis in Dr. Labuschagne's chapter. Scientific and medical research has so much to gain by recognizing these similarities. And scripture suggests that a careful study of animal behaviour offers much to challenge and instruct aspects of our own ways of living and behaving.

I conclude by offering two specific comments as a scientist who is also a Christian. First, when you are considering the possibility of differences between animals and humans, there are important scientific issues involved. For example, when someone suffers brain damage it is usually difficult to know precisely what structures have been damaged. It is therefore unwise to make strong conclusions about the functions of brain structures from clinical material alone. It is important when studying the function(s) of a particular part of the brain, to augment the clinical evidence by studying the effects of careful surgical ablations on the brains of animals. Such methods minimise unwanted damage and therefore make it safer to draw conclusions about specialised function. It seems to me, as a Christian, that the humane use of animals in such research is proper. But, as Cas Labuschagne emphasises "The human being owes this privileged position not to himself, but to God who endows him with the capability and the competence to rule and have dominion over other living creatures" and that "There is no room here for human haughtiness, for arrogance .... for a feeling of superiority above other living beings. Humans owe their high status not to themselves, but to God whom they are called to serve by ruling over God's other creatures on earth." It is thus clear to me that in this regard exercising our stewardship requires the minimum use of animals and as far as possible the exclusion of suffering.

My second comment is that I find little encouragement in the Bible for trying to establish the distinctiveness of humankind on the basis of certain physical or mental traits. That being so the question remains, what is it that is distinctive? The key to what it means to be distinctively human is not to be found in looking for every possible physical and mental difference between ourselves and the animal kingdom. Rather the crucial clues for the Christian are to be found in scripture.

One such is identified by Cas Labuschagne in the following chapter and is found in Genesis chapters 1 and 2. Dr. Labuschagne points out that "The human being is fundamentally a breathing, living creature like other creatures". He then goes on to identify the difference which provides our first clue when he writes "The difference, however, between human and animal, according to our author, is that *it is only in the human being that God breaths the 'breath of life'* (nishmat chayyah)" (my italics). And this he adds "... seems to stress the unique relationship between the human being and God, and functions as a parallel to the idea of humankind being created in the image of God". Man, uniquely has the potential for a personal relationship with his Creator, Father, God. He may "walk with Him in the cool of the evening". A relationship which, however marred by disobedience, is gloriously restored in Christ - and that leads on to our second clue.

The second clue and for me the pre-eminent one comes from the Incarnation. As another biblical scholar has written, "The most remarkable fact about the human race, as we learn from the Bible, is that a genuinely human life, the fully perfect human personality of the historic existence of Jesus, served as a mode of existence of God Himself without ceasing in the least to be fully God". "If human life is a vehicle equal to that task," he wrote, "it is glorious indeed." These it seems to me are firmer grounds for recognizing our special status than looking for psychological and structural differences.

There will then always be a delicate balance to be maintained. Pascal, I believe, had it about right when he wrote, "It is dangerous to show man too clearly how much he resembles the beast, without at the same time showing him his greatness. It is also dangerous to allow him too clear a vision of his greatness without his baseness. It is even more dangerous to leave him in ignorance of both."

8

Creation and the Status of Humanity in the Bible

Cas J. Labuschagne (Groningen)

The purpose of this paper is to present the biblical doctrine of the creation of human beings, and to study its implications for the status of humanity in relation to the rest of the universe, especially in relation to other living creatures. Since I am a biblical scholar, my contribution to the consultation will be an exposition of what the creation-texts say about the issue. One of the most important texts is the first chapter of Genesis (1:1 - 2:3), the only comprehensive story of creation in the Bible. It functions as a prologue to the biblical (hi)story of humankind (Gen. 2:4ff.).

The second chapter of Genesis has traditionally been interpreted as a 'second (different) story of creation', supposed to have belonged to a separate literary source. However, Genesis 2 is not a creation story, but should be understood as part of the primeval history of humankind in the garden of Eden (Gen. 2:4 - 3:24), in which the garden symbolically represents the natural environment of human beings. In presenting his view on the primeval history of humankind the author of the story made ample use of a variety of creation motives, but this does not make the story a creation story.

In addition to Genesis 1 and 2 we shall study briefly a few other relevant texts such as Psalm 8 and 104 amongst others, in order to get an overall view of what the Bible teaches about the position of human beings in relation to other living creatures and to the rest of the universe.

The theocentric view of creation and the modest position of humanity

One of the most deplorable misconceptions with regard to the biblical doctrine of creation is that creation is usually considered to be anthropocentric. Humankind is supposed to be the 'crown' of God's creation and the ultimate purpose of creation. There is, however, no biblical basis for this arrogant claim, which is certainly of Greek origin, being adopted from Greek philosophy by the early fathers of the Christian church.

The view that humankind is the 'crown' of God's creation cannot be based upon the fact that the creation of human beings is the last and supreme act of creation in Genesis 1. The fact of the matter, however, is that human beings are created on the very same day as the rest of the living creatures on the earth, i.e. on the sixth day. The main reason why the creation of the creatures living on the ground (including human beings) is situated by the author on the last day of creation, is a literary one: to obtain an open end to the creation story: these creatures are going to be the main subjects in 'the story of the heavens and the earth after their creation' in Gen. 2:4ff. The special status of human beings in relation to other creatures in Gen. 1:26f. does not render them the 'crown' of God's creation either.

Moreover, the idea in Gen. 2:8 that God planted a garden in Eden, and that He put in it the human being (the man) He had created, cannot be interpreted to mean that the garden was specially created for the benefit of humankind. On the contrary, the relationship between the man and the garden is rather one of mutual dependence. The garden is there for the man, and he is there for the garden: the man is put in the garden 'to till it and look after it' (2:15). In relation to his natural environment the human being is nothing but a humble servant, an agricultural labourer. What is more, the garden is not his property, since it belongs to God.

Far from being anthropocentric, the biblical view of creation is *theocentric*. The creation is God's, and the ultimate purpose of creation is not humanity, but rather the embodiment and expression of God's greatness and majesty in the universe. Significantly enough the purpose of both Psalm 8 and 104, the two psalms of creation, is primarily to praise the majesty and splendour of the Creator, who is said to rejoice in his works. In Psalm 104 it is said:

'Lord my God, you are very great, clothed in majesty and splendour and
enfolded in a robe of light' (vs. 1f.) and 'May the glory of the Lord stand
for ever, and may the Lord rejoice in his works' (vs. 31).

When the psalmist enumerates God's acts of creation, which are in fact the acts of a continuous creation (*creatio continua*), in which God provides for all his creatures, a very modest position is allotted to humanity. Man is mentioned not before, but after the cattle in vss. 14ff. :

'You make grass grow for the cattle and plants for the use of mortals, producing food from the earth, and wine to gladden the heart of man, oil to make his face shine, and bread to strengthen man's heart' (see also Psalm 148:7-13).

And speaking about the sun and the moon, day and night, in vss. 19-23, the author of Ps. 104 refers to humanity only in passing:

'Man goes out to his work and his labours until evening'.

In Psalm 19:1-6 in which it is stated that 'the heavens tell out the glory of God', human beings are not even mentioned.

The modest position of humanity in the universe is expressed in an unequivocal way in Psalm 8, which begins and ends with the words:

'Lord our sovereign, how glorious is your name throughout the world' (vss. 1 and 9).

Contemplating the position of man in God's creation the psalmist says:

'When I look up at your heavens, the work of your fingers, at the moon and the stars you have set in place, what is a frail mortal, that you should be mindful of him, a human being, that you shall take notice of him?' (vss. 3f.; see also Ps. 144:3f.).

The context, in which the psalmist speaks about the high status of humanity, is the universe. The extraordinary position of the human being in comparison with other living creatures, is set against the backdrop of the author's amazement about God's vast creation, and about his care for humankind as an infinitively small object in the universe.

The high status of the human being is defined as 'being little short of divine': God has made him 'little less than a god, crowning him with glory and honour' (vs. 5). The human being owns this privileged position not to himself, but to God who endows him with the capability and the competence to rule and have dominion over other living creatures:

'You make him master over all that you have made, putting everything in subjection under his feet: all sheep and oxen, all the wild beasts, the birds in the air, the fish in the sea, and everything that moves along ocean paths' (vss. 6-8).

The human being is given his high status not for his own sake, but in view of his divine commission to be master over other living creatures. There is no room here for human haughtiness, for arrogance or for a feeling of superiority above other living beings. Humans owe their high status not to themselves, but to God, whom they are called to serve by ruling over God's other creatures on earth.

This idea of the human being's dominion over other creatures is expressed in the creation story by means of the notion that human beings are created 'in the image of God':

> 'Let us make human beings in our image, after our likeness, to have dominion over the fish in the sea, the birds of the air, the cattle, all wild animals on land, and everything that creeps on the earth' (Gen. 1:26).

Scholars rightly maintain that the essential meaning of the phrase 'in the image of God' is explained in what is said about God's purpose with his creating humans in his image, namely that they should have dominion over the other creatures. The analogy between God and the human being exists primarily in the competence and the capability of humans to rule and to have dominion over other living creatures. Being created in God's image, however, does not render humans into absolute rulers that lord it over everything else. On the contrary, the human being is destined by God to rule, but he is not the supreme ruler - he is not a god, but one of God's creatures.

In the creation story human rulership over the other creatures is *limited* in a significant way, in that humans are not explicitly allowed to kill other creatures for food. God gives human beings for food 'all seed-bearing plants and all fruit and seed-bearing trees'. He provides for other living creatures by giving them for food 'all green plants' (1:29f.). The author of the creation story has an ideal situation in mind in which there is no room for carnivores. This ideal situation corresponds with the eschatological expectation in the messianic age, when

> 'the wolf will live with the lamb, and the leopard lie down with the kid; the calf and the young lion feed together, with a little child to tend them; the cow and the bear will be friends, their young will lie together and the lion will eat straw like cattle... there will be neither hurt nor harm... (Is. 11:6ff.).

It is only after the loss of paradise, more specifically after the flood, that there is fear-and-dread of humans among the animals (Gen. 9:2), and that humans are given other living creatures for food (vs. 3). There is, however, a severe *restriction*: they are not allowed to eat flesh with its life, i.e. its blood still in it (vs. 4). Man's competence to kill for food is limited: he is not allowed to destroy the essence of life or life itself, since it belongs to God only. Thus the dominion of the human being over other creatures is limited. That reminds us of St. Paul's words setting out the limits for Christian behaviour:

> 'Everything belongs to you... all are yours, but you belong to Christ, and Christ to God' (I Cor. 3:22).

Humanity in ecological perspective

Turning now to the creation motives in the story of the garden of Eden in Genesis 2, we may observe that, in contradistinction to Genesis 1, where God and his creation are set in a cosmological perspective, the author here focuses his attention upon the human being in ecological perspective. The story can be characterized as an anthropological narrative, the issue being the man in his natural environment, his relation with God, the earth, the animals and his fellow-man, the woman. The main character in the story is the individual male human being, whom God 'formed from the dust of the ground', in whose nostrils God 'breathed the breath of life, so that he became a living creature' (2:7, cf. Job 34:13-15).[1]

The idea of God breathing the breath of life in the man's nostrils presents the human being as a 'living creature', i.e. a being that is more than 'living matter'. Significantly enough the author uses the same term, 'living creature' (*nephesh chayyah*) as in Gen. 1:24,30, where it designates the animals. The human being is fundamentally a breathing, living creature like other living creatures. The difference, however, between human and animal, according to our author, is that it is only in the human being that God breathes the 'breath of life' (*nishmat chayyah*). This motive seems to stress the unique relationship between the human being and God, and functions as a parallel to the idea of humankind being created in the image of God.

By the way, the idea that there is a fundamental difference between human beings and animals is seriously questioned by the Speaker in the book of Ecclesiastes, whose merit was that he questioned and challenged the theological axioms of his time:

> 'I said to myself, 'In dealing with human beings it is God's purpose to test them and to see what they truly are. Human beings and beasts share one and the same fate: death comes to both alike. They all draw the same breath. Man has no advantage over beast, for everything is futility. All go to the same place: all came from the dust, and to dust all return. Who knows whether the spirit of a human being goes upward or whether the spirit of a beast goes downward to the earth?'' (Eccl. 3:18-21).

In Genesis 2 the human being is presented as an *earth*-man by means of the motive of the dust as the raw material from which the man is created. The words *'adam*, 'man', and *'adamah*, 'earth', are etymologically related. The human being

---

1. For a recent thorough treatment of the story, see E. J. van Wolde, *A Semiotic Analysis of Genesis 2-3* (Studia Semitica Neerlandica 25) Assen 1989, especially 121-209.

is 'taken from the earth' and will in the end 'return to the earth' (3:19). The relationship between the human being and the earth is one of mutual dependence: the earth (ground) depends upon humans who till it and look after it; and humans on their part need, depend upon, and are responsible for the earth for their existence.

The relationship between humans and animals

The relationship between human beings and animals, and between man and his fellow-man, is the theme of the next phase in the story. History cannot begin before the issue of relationships is resolved. History is impossible without procreation, and procreation depends upon the right relationships. In God's sight the individual's 'being alone' is 'not good' - the first 'not good' after the series of 'God saw that it was good' in the creation story. The individual human being should have (literally) 'an equivalent over against him', i.e. a 'partner suited to him' (so rightly the *Revised English Bible*). The traditional rendering 'a helper fit for him' - so the *Revised Standard Version* - is not only wrong, but has also led to the most unfortunate misconception with regard to the position of women, as if the female is nothing more than the helper of the male. In this view of the female the fundamental equality of male and female, clearly implied in Gen. 1:26f., is being totally disregarded. It has caused suffering and misery to women through the ages until the present day.

In order to retard the resolution of the issue of a suitable partner in view of procreation, the author of Genesis 2 let God conduct an experiment in order to explain the relationship between human beings and animals: God creates the animals and confronts the man with them to see how he will react and call them. The man 'named' all living creatures, i.e. he exerts his dominion over the animals. Name-giving is an act of mastering, ruling, controlling and commanding. The relationship is anything but a partnership, as our author explicitly states: 'for the man himself no suitable partner was found' among the animals (2:20). Conversely, the human being cannot be a partner of the animals, his fellow-'living creatures', since he is a living creature of another order, being created in God's image, having received the breath of life, and being endowed with a vast potential of possibilities and with spiritual qualities lacking in animals.[2] This is the reason why there were clear barriers and limits in ancient Israel with regard to the relationship between humans and animals: they were not allowed to 'know' each other; sexual intercourse was strictly forbidden and bestiality was abhorred.

---

2.   See on this point Malcolm Jeeves' paper.

128

The human being can have only another human being as partner. The example par excellence of human partnership is the partnership of male and female, which does not of course exclude partnerships between males and between females.

In biblical law the relationship between humans and animals was based upon mercifulness, humanity (humane-ness) and consideration. Working cattle were granted the right to rest on the Sabbath; the Israelites had to take care of a straying donkey and had to help an animal lying helpless under its load (Ex. 23:4-5). They were not to muzzle an ox while it was treading out the grain (Deut. 25:4; cf. I Cor. 9:9). They had to respect the continuing process of life in the animal world, by not taking from the nest both the mother bird and her young (Deut. 22:6f.). They were not allowed to slaughter a cow or sheep at the same time as its young, i.e. killing two generations simultaneously (Lev. 22:28). Boiling a kid in its mother's milk was strictly forbidden (Ex. 23:19; 34:26 and Deut. 14:21).

On the whole in biblical times the relationship between humans and animals was ambivalent: on the one hand the Israelites had respect and sympathy for animals that were not considered dangerous and did not form a menace. The dog is an exception, since it was despised in biblical times, in contradistinction to the fact that in our culture at the present time the dog is the most popular pet according to a recent inquiry in the USA.[3] On the other hand people in biblical times feared and showed aggression towards beasts regarded as dangerous, such as snakes, lions and bears, or as awe-inspiring, such as the crocodile and the hippopotamus. They had either to kill such animals or flee from them in order to survive in the dangerous and menacing environment in which they were living.

The issue of survival
Allow me in conclusion to make a few remarks about the issue of survival. Nature does not only know the law of the survival of the fittest within one species, but also the law of the survival of the strongest or the cleverest among different creatures when it comes to 'eat or be eaten'. Human beings have

---

3.   See S.R. Kellert, Perceptions of Animals in America, in R.J.Hoage (ed.), *Perceptions of Animals in American Culture* (Washington D.C. 1989), 5-24. I owe this reference and those in the three following notes to J.J. Boersema, "Waarom is een poedel 'een ding'...?", paper read at the congress "Ethiek tussen theorie en praktijk", held on 15-16 November 1990 at the Free University of Amsterdam (to be published soon). I might also mention his paper "Eerst de Jood, maar ook de Griek; op zoek naar de wortels van het milieuprobleem in de westerse cultuur", to be published in W. Zweers (ed.), *Eerst de Jood, maar ook de Griek.*

survived until now probably because they have proved themselves to be the cleverest creatures. At the present time humans do not have a single natural enemy that forms a threat to their survival. On the other hand we humans have formed and do still form a menace to many animals either by hunting them down, or by the exploitation of land and forests, or simply by our way of life in which many creatures have either become extinct or simply cannot survive for long. Our own survival in the historic sense of the word is no longer at stake, but the survival of many fellow-creatures is certainly at stake.

Hasn't the time come to make the right of survival an important political and theological issue for our time? Shouldn't we recognize and state categorically that *all creatures* have the right to survive? Whatever our answer may be, we have to admit that up till now human beings have monopolized the right of survival. When we recognize and fight for human rights, shouldn't we recognize and exert ourselves for the rights of other living creatures as well? I do not imply that moral rights should be extended to animals.[4] That is not the point. What we have to do is restrict human rights with regard to animals,[5] and recognize the animals' right of survival. The point at issue is not moral rights, but the *right of survival* of all species. This right can be based *morally* upon the inherent (c.q. intrinsic) value of every living creature,[6] and *theologically* upon the integrity of creation as the embodiment and manifestation of the majesty and glory of God the Creator. The time is ripe for the universal acceptance of the right of survival for all living species, and for serious political measures to be taken by all countries in the world on the basis of the 'United Nations Charter for Nature, adopted by the General Assembly in 1982.[7]

Isn't it significant - and I now return to the book of Genesis - that during the flood Noah's ark was not only for humans a haven of survival, but for 'all living creatures of every kind, birds, beasts and creeping things' (cf. e.g. Gen. 8:17f.)? Theologically speaking, therefore, humans have no right whatsoever to

---

4. This is the view of P.Singer, *Animal Liberation. A new Ethics for our Treatment of Animals* (London 1976).

5. See J. Passmore, "The treatment of animals", *Journal of the History of Ideas* 36 (1975), 195-218; especially 217.

6. For these terms see B. Devall and G. Sessions (eds.), *Deep Ecology* (Salt Lake City 1985).

7. See Günter Altner, *Naturvergessenheit: Grundlage einer umfassende Bioethik*, Darmstadt 1991, especially the chapter 'Bioethik und Schöpfungstheologie' on pp. 73-115, more specifically pp. 101ff.; for the relevant German literature see pp. 294f.

monopolize the right of survival. God's concern is not only with human beings, but with all his creatures!

May I remind the theologically minded among us that the biblical idea of *covenant* in the broadest sense of the word is the post-diluvian covenant between God and the descendants of Noah *and* 'every living creature that is with you, all birds and cattle, all the animals with you on earth' (Gen. 9:8f.). This covenant is anything but anthropocentric - it is clearly *ecocentric*. Why have we humans monopolized that covenant by making it anthropocentric, eclipsing God's other creatures?

And finally, I might refer to St. Paul's *cosmic* view of the reconciliation in Christ. In the letter to the Colossians he says:

'(Christ) is the image of the invisible God; his is the primacy over all creation... for in him God in all his fullness chose to dwell, and through him to reconcile *all things* to himself... *all things*, whether on earth or in heaven' (1:15-20).

The reconciliation in Christ, which we Christians have monopolized by making it relevant only to human beings, is in fact ecocentric, if not biocentric, since it encompasses all things.

9

The Ecological Crisis
and Creation Theology

Martin Palmer (Manchester)

It may seem like a bold statement, but I believe the human race faces the real risk of pushing itself and much of creation into a post-evolutionary stage of creation. We are so rapidly speeding up the natural processes of creation - the cycle of evolution, change, death and new birth, that we are seriously in danger of overtaking the normal processes of creation and creating a world in our own image. That will be a damaged, strained, polluted world - not the world I believe the Creator wishes.

If the human race is not to enter into a post-evolutionary stage of creation, we need to find new maps of our world, of our universe and these maps have little to do with geography. We need new maps of our minds which help us to understand our place and if there is one, our purpose within creation, otherwise, we shall drive ourselves and many other species to the point, beyond evolution and creation - into the post-evolutionary world of human destruction and mutation.

What do I mean by the maps? Let me tell you a story which captures the consequences in action of two very different maps of meaning of our world.

In 1953 two men reached the top of Mount Everest. One was the Western explorer scientist Edmund Hillary. The other was Tenzing Norgay, the guide from the Buddhist hill community of the Sherpas. When Hillary reached the top, he stuck a Union Jack into the snow and proclaimed that he had "conquered" the mountain. Sherpa Tenzing knelt in the snow and prayed for forgiveness from the gods of the mountain for having disturbed them.

Let us descend from the heights of Mount Everest. As we do so today, we shall pass mountains - of rubbish. We will pass places where certain fragile ecosystems have been completely destroyed by the tourists who now crowd the mountain. As we descend even further, into the tree belt of the Himalayas, we will find that there is now virtually no forest left. Deforestation has swept the ancient mountains clean of their woods, taking with them many sepcies, including ones we never even knew existed. From our vantage point we can see the rivers of the Himalayas churning brown through the valleys as they carry away the topsoil which has sustained the fragile balance of life in these great valleys for millenia.

To see the fruits of the destruction by logging of the forests of the Himalayas, we need to travel along the swollen riverways to Bangladesh, where devastating floods have resulted from the waters washing off the hills and the silting up of the delta.

Or we could follow another great explorer, Thor Heyerdahl who in the late 40s undertook his epic journey across the Pacific. In the early 70s he repeated the journey. To his horror something had changed. In the 40s, once he was two or three days away from the mainland, he saw no signs of humanity. In the 70s, there was not a single hour which passed, even in the midst of the Pacific, when they did not sail past human rubbish such as plastic, oil slicks or tins.

This fouling of our nest is but one feature of what we are doing to the environment. Through the massive increase in farming, deforestation, industry and domestic factors such as cars, refrigerators and hair sprays, we are producing an ever thickening field of virtually indestructable gases around the planet. This thickening field prevents the escape of heat from the planet. The effect is like building a glasshouse over the entire planet. The result is a rapidly increasing temperature over the entire globe. With this increase in temperature, totally without precedence in the history of the planet because it is happening over a matter of years rather than tens of thousands of years, the seas are also rising. They have risen world wide by 15cm since the start of the century. They will rise by almost twice that much before the end of the century, even if we were to stop adding to the greenhouse effect today. The impact of this on a world in which half the world's population lives in low lying land areas will be truly catastrophic. This is not just scaremongering. When the public inquiry was being held into the planned building of a new nuclear power station at Hinkley Point in the UK in March 1989, the Chief Scientist of the UK, David Fisk, pointed out a weakness in the plans. The Thames Barrier which would hold back flood waters from reaching the station, was built to contain up to a 30cm rise in general sea level over the next century. It is now expected, said Mr. Fisk, that this will in fact be reached within twenty years.

I could go on. About deforestation and the loss of over half of the forests since the end of the 60s; of the loss, the extinction, of over 10,000 species every year since the end of the 70s; of the apparently inexorable movement of the great deserts such as the Sahara - one of the main reasons behind the Ethiopian and Sudan famines of the mid and late 80s, and a legacy of the West's first major ecological crisis, over-farming by the late Roman Empire; of the death of over 20,000 lakes in Sweden by last year due to acid rain. I could spell out for you the already visible consequences of our vast experiment with life itself on this planet - an experiment which is going drastically wrong and over which we seem to have little control and even less care. We could look at the way in which we have speeded up the normal processes of evolution to such a point that we have broken the evolutionary barrier and have now taken over as the agents of world change, leaving evolutionary processes in ruins.

But statistics are quite frankly meaningless, unless set within a context of moral and ethical concern, rooted in beliefs which can not only comprehend this data, but begin to construct new ways of response. For at its heart, the ecological crisis is a crisis of the mind, more than it is a crisis of resources.

The ecological movement is, to a considerable degree, a child or grandchild of the Judaeo-Christian-Islamic tradition. For at its heart, it is apocalyptic. When facts pile in and swamp us, it is to apocalyptic language that people in the environmental movement turn. The movement accepts without question the linear model of time. As such it is heir to the Judaeo-Christian Islamic belief that what arises at a given point from (in Christian thought) nothing, will eventually end and dissolve into nothingness. What starts at A will have to end at Z. It accepts without question that the extinction or dramatic diminution of the human race would be terrible. It turns to the Book of Revelation to find its terminology, from the horrific descriptions of the polluting of the waters, and the fires that burn up a third of the world, to that powerful sentence in Chapter 11 "the time has come to destroy those who are destroying the earth." In its desire to convince us of the urgency of the crisis, it paints for us a picture of the end of the world - in just the same way as Chistianity has used the end of time and the Judgement Day - to try and engender moral behaviour.

It is forceful language and imagery. Christianity has taught us to see time as linear with a beginning and end - a meaning and a purpose. In our models and maps of reality we have been told that nothing lasts for ever. Furthermore, we

134

have been taught by our faith that at the end of time, God will end this planet, and in the wonderful words of Revelation

"Then I saw a new heaven and a new earth; the first heaven and the first earth had disappeared now, and there was no longer any sea.

I saw the holy city, and the new Jerusalen, coming down from God out of heaven, as beautiful as a bride all dressed for her husband.

Then I heard a loud voice call from the throne, 'You see this city? Here God lives among men. He will make his home among them; they shall be his people, and he will be their God; his name is God-with-them.

He will wipe away all tears from their eyes; there will be no more death, and no more mourning and sadness. The world of the past has gone.'

The the One sitting on the throne spoke: 'Now I am making the whole of creation new' he said, 'Write this: that what I am saying is sure and will come true.'"

Rev 21:1-5

According to the Biblical tradition, the end of time, of history, of this planet, will be a moral act by the Ground of our Being, by God in God's infinite wisdom and in God's own time. What we are now confronting, so many ecologists and other "doomsters" tell us, is the possible end of time, the end of history, the end of the process of natural evolution of this planet as a result of the stupidity and arrogance of humanity; a humanity which plays god but without moral point and purpose - without the ability to replace that which is lost with something new and glorious.

It is this playing at being God that lies at the heart of the ecological crisis. This is why theology, or to be more honest, the faith of the church is so vital to coping with the ecological crisis. The crisis is a crisis of concepts and not just about use. For how we treat the world depends on what we believe. To give just two examples from the most extreme ends. James Watt, the former American secretary of the Interior - responsible for the environment in the last Government of President Reagan - is a born again Christian. He believes that Christ will return within the next decade. As secretary with responsibility for the environment he was quite prepared to allow unlimited and unrestrained exploitation of the national parks, coastline and so forth of the USA. The reason? If Jesus is comining within the next twenty years, why bother to keep anything in its pristine condition? Jesus will create it all anew anyway! This man was in charge of national conservation policy.

In the Jain faith, Jain monks and nuns sweep the road before them to save any little creatures from being trodden upon and killed by accident. The roots of this lie in a belief in total non-violence and commonality of the divine spark within each and every manifestation of creation. Yet even here, events have caught up with the Jains, calling for a new theology and map of our purpose here. Traditionally Jain layfolk have gone into trades which did no harm to living entities. Thus they eschewed farming, the meat trade, working with leather or other such practices and went instead into areas such as diamonds, mining and early chemical studies for these were not living souls. Now they have just awoken to the fact that these trades are amongst the worst offenders against the environment and that mining and chemcals are no longer acceptable areas of work. They are having to redraw their maps of reality. They are having to face the cost of divesting themselves of these trades, or of bearing responsibility for the death of millions of creatures. It is not easy, but at least they have started.

Religion therefore can provide both ways forward but also ways backwards. Much of the ethical teaching of the past is simply unable to handle the realities of today and even if the broad principles hold true, we need to radicaly alter the outworkings of them.

The question we have to address therefore as a theological gathering of predominatly Christian hue is, does Christianity help or hinder the survival of creation, the integrity of creation, by the beliefs it teaches and by its practices? Is it, as some have argued, the very cause of the ecological crisis because it de-sacralises nature and elevates humanity above nature? Or is it the place wherein we can rediscover or reclaim the original vision of humanity in nature which can actually take us, conceptually, out of this crisis?

I want to argue that both are true.

Christianity, along with its related faiths, Judaism, Islam, Marxism, rationalistic science and so forth, all have a distinct teaching. In some way, humanity is both a part of creation and apart from creation. In the Christian story, we are the final product; the only species created specifically by God (the rest are called forth from the land, sea or air) and the only one to be in the likeness of God. Furthermore, through the power of naming and through the 'gift' of 'domination', we are given authority and power which sets us apart from creation.

Islam is even more explicit about this than Christianity. According to the Qur'an and Hadith, we do not belong to this planet. The Garden was another planet. The Fall was literally that. Adam fell to earth from another planet, which is why you can go and see where his foot hit the ground on Adam's Peak in Sri Lanka.

Judaism gives us a very interesting perspective. It always strikes me as sad that Christianity only took the synopsis of Judaism - the Torah - without also taking the fuller stories as recorded in the Talmud. In the Talmud we are told how the angels protested when God announced he was going to make humanity to put on his new planet. They pointed out that this planet was pretty good, not perfect, but nevertheless pretty good. Why spoil it with human beings? A great row broke out, which was only resolved when the Earth spoke up and said she would care for humanity if they respected her.

Genesis 1 and 2 have a lot to be blamed for, and one thing which it can be blamed for is having given us a very elevated view of our own importance. We have read the story of salvation history as a purely human event. Yet look at the first covenant God ever makes. The covenant with Noah. But is it just with Noah? Far from it. It is with Noah, with his descendants, with

> "every living creature to be found with you, birds, cattle and every wild beast with you, everything that came out of the ark, everything that lives on the earth."
>
> Genesis 9:9-10

Salvation history has been treated as the story of God and humanity. The rest of creation has been taken as a colourful backdrop, a stage prop against which the drama of humanity has been acted out. This is where Christianity in some of its expressions has led us astray. This is where the arrogance of humanity has usurped the stage of life from the others in the cast of creation. The cosmological intentions of the first Covenant have been lost, or abandoned by humanity, and frequently by both the Church and theology. God's world has lost its divinity and we have elevated human needs and human interests to be the central point, and purpose, of creation. In doing so we have dislodged both the rest of Creation, and now God.

The effects of this can be seen in the arguments so often put forward to justify conservation of the environment because it is useful to us. The environment has meaning and purpose not because of its inherent right to exist as part of God's creation, but because we give it meaning by using it. Let us look at an example of this thinking. Read, for instance, the core philosophy of the World Conservation Strategy, drawn up in 1980:

> "1. The aim of the World Conservation Strategy is to achieve the three main objectives of living resource conservation:

a. to maintain essential ecological processes and life-support systems (such as soil) regeneration and protection, the recycling of nutrients, and the cleansing of waters), on which human survival and development depend;

b. to preserve genetic diversity (the range of genetic material found in the world's organisms), on which depend the functioning of many of the above processes and life-support systems, the breeding programmes necessary for the protection and improvement of cultivated plants, domesticated animals and micro-organisms, as well as much scientific and medical advance, technical innovations, and the security of the many industries that use living resources;

c. to ensure the sustainable utilization of species and ecosystems (notably fish and other wildlife, forests and grazing lands), which support millions of rural communities as well as major industries."

(World Conservation Strategy, published by IUCN-UNEP-WWFM 1980)

All life is judged in terms of its utilization by us - that is what the WCS states. Perhaps an example of the outcome of this way of thinking might be helpful. The armadillo is found only in the jungles of America. It was nearly wiped out ten years ago. Then it was discovered that armadillos are the only creatures in the world other than humans to suffer from leprosy. It was also discovered that if you injected leprosy into the footpad of the armadillo, it produces a reaction from which a serum can be made which cures leprosy in humans. And thank God for that. But, the argument goes, imagine what a loss to humanity it would have been if the armadillo had been made extinct before we discovered this! Well, yes. But maybe the armadillo would have something to say about being made extinct!

But let us just pursue this a bit further. What we are actually saying is that millions of years of evolution has taken place so that we can turn the poor amadillo upside down and stick a pin in its foot! What arrogance. What conceit to evaluate the value of a species by its usefulness to us. To say in effect that it has no meaning or purpose unless we use it. I am reminded of that splendid limerick,

> There was a young man who said, "God
> To you it must seem very odd,
> That this tree as a tree
> Simply ceases to be
> When there is no-one about in the quad."

"Dear Sir, it is not at all odd.
I am always about in the quad,
And the tree as a tree
Continues to be,
Observed by yours faithfully, God."

It is the same arrogance as is to be found in the story I began with. For a human being, part of a species a couple of million years old, to climb a mountain and sticking a flag in it, claim that he has conquered it - shows what a world of delusion we live in. It also shows us why our attitude to nature has got us into such deep ecological trouble.

The tendency towards anthropocentrism in Christianity is indeed a major cause I would contend, of the current ecological crisis. We pride ourselves as post renaissance people that we are heirs of the Copernicus revolution. Not for us, we say, the fable that the earth is at the centre of the universe, around which all else circles, has its centre and thus its meaning. But this is simply not true. We may have removed the earth from the centre of our understanding of the universe, but we have left humanity firmly there. It is around us, we believe, that life circles, has its centre and its meaning. The dangers of this we can now see staring us in the face. Our anthropocentrism has murdered millions of species in such a short time that the normal processes of evolution, in which millions of species come and go, can no longer keep up, nor ensure the successful evolution of new species. As a species, we need salvation. Salvation from our sins and from our arrogation of the meaning of creation.

This is where traditionally expressed concepts of salvation are inadequate. We have turned salvation from a universal phenomenon, into a purely human event. We have not only ignored the cosmic context set by the first covenant, but have ignored even St Paul's definition of why Christ died upon the cross.

"He is the image of the unseen God
and the first born of all creation,
for in him were created
all things in heaven and on earth;
everything visible and everything invisible .....

As he is the Beginning
he was the first to be born from the dead,
so that he should be perfect in every way;
because God wanted all perfection

to be found in him
and all things to be reconciled through him and for him,
everything in heaven and everything on earth,
when he made peace
by his death upon the cross."

Col. 1:15-20.

We have lost sight of the fact that "God so loved the world - [kosmos] - that he sent his only Son". Not just humanity, but the kosmos, the ordered universe of creation. We have reduced the redemption wrought by Christ on the tree from a cosmic event to a human drama. Having been taught a faith which appeared to maintain that we had the right to usurp creation from its place in the affections of the Creator - and you only have to read the psalms or Job 38-39 to see how God revels in all creation - can we really express surprise when this self same conceited humanity then usurps God from the centre of history and meaning, and enthrones itself there and begins to move, inexorably as many would see it, to the final blasphemy of trying to end time and creation?

The ecological crisis is a crisis of faith. As the source of that crisis, Christianity has to look long and hard at what it has done and it has to see what has been lost. What we have lost or broken is the integrity of God's creation, for by placing ourselves so firmly apart from creation, we have learnt to scorn the rest of creation.

In modern Western Christian thought, recognition of this split and the damage it has created, has led us to explore those very troubling verses in Genesis about domination and putting fear into the rest of creation. We have come up with terms such as dominion means stewardship, or that we are meant to be trustees. These phrases are all very well, but they leave the key problem unresolved. For we still see ourselves as separate from the rest of creation. The terms we use are managerial, remote from feeling, manipulative. They fail to resolve the divide we have created.

Some argue that we should forget altogether about our special role in creation. But this is foolish. For better or for worse, whether because of what God ordained or because of the way we have perceived ourselves from our reading of Scripture, we operate as no other species operates. We do now have power or authority over all other species. So how do we reconcile this? How do we deal with our distinctiveness from the rest of creation, and with the fact of our communality with the rest of creation? Not, I would argue, by stumbling around with words such as "steward" or "trustee".

It is within the wisdom of the Orthodox Church that I believe we can find some form of model which begins to help us with this crisis of the mind - crisis of the environment.

The image used by the Orthodox to describe our relationship to both God and the rest of creation, is priesthood. I realise that this phrase has become most powerfully charged for many of us in the churches today. But I would ask you to bear with the term, and to view it as covering all of us, not just those who happen to be male.

The image of the priesthood of creation is understood thus. When a priest stands before God at the altar and offers the bread and wine, s/he does so in no right of his/her own. The bread and the wine have not been made by the priest. They are the fruits of the people. Likewise, when the priest offers the consecrated bread and wine back to the people, s/he offers nothing from his/herself. The gift of bread and wine is a sign of grace, which has not been earned by the priest nor is confined to the priest. It is given of God for the blessing and fulfilment of all. The priest is simply and yet gloriously the one who makes this interaction possible.

So, say the Orthodox, should our relationship be with the rest of creation. As the most articulate form of creation, we can offer to God the fruits of creation in their fullness. We are not the whole of creation, but we can be the conduit for creation to speak to its creator. Likewise, we can be the vehicle for God's grace to creation. Grace is not just for us, but is a gift for all life. Perhaps what best describes this relationship is the term, 'servant priest', carrying with it both the notion of authority but also of service. A tension which we need to see in our role of domination in nature as described by Genesis.

When viewed this way, the arrogation to ourselves of God's grace and the placing of ourselves at the centre of meaning and purpose in creation, is seen for what it is. Robbery and deceit. Worse, it is done through gross misuse of the unique and privileged position which we have. Try a simple experiment in your own home area. Look around there and see if you can find anything in your area which speaks to you of humanity acting as a vehicle of grace, as a blessing, to the rest of nature. I expect you will be able to find plenty of examples of dominion, of abuse of stewardship - but of blessing? Try it and see!

In this paper, I have deliberately spoken in images and models. For this is how we actually operate. The story of meaning which we construct for ourselves creates the way we behave. There can be no doubt that the world cannot afford for us to continue with the present models. The quest is for new models. In conventional environmental language, there is a constant call for "new ethics". But that is impossible for ethics do not appear just like that. They can only grow out of a set of convictions, which in themselves can only emerge naturally from a set of fundamental beliefs. And such beliefs only work if they help us construct a framework of meaning which keeps the awe-full-ness of the universe from crushing us by its apparent meaninglessness. Furthermore, most talk in conservation circles of a new ethics simply means trying to find ways of moderating our destructive habits - not of fundamentally challenging or altering them. I would claim that we actually need to rediscover the original model as revealed within God's salvationary action in history and his liberating power in Christ. We need to find our special place, but not at the expense of the integrity of the rest of creation or indeed at the expense of the integrity of God.

The ecological movement itself operates through symbol and myth. As I have indicated, much of this derives from the Judaeo-Christian-Islamic background from which it has sprung. The environmental movement is essentially a Western creation. Motivated by the pervasive imagery of Revelation, and driven by the Biblical view of linear time, the environmental movement has sought to disturb, shock and then bribe us into action. Yet this has largely failed. The attempt to disturb us had its roots in the 1950's. As the impact of modern farming, forestry, industry and development began to be felt, so the response was to try and create sanctuaries where certain species could be left in peace. Don't forget, most people were unaware of the true extent of environmental damage at this time, and the great attack on the rainforests only began in the mid 60's.

Soon however, it became obvious that we needed to be more than just disturbed about the threats to certain species. For it became obvious that nature does not operate in neat, definable areas. The shock of discovering that a bird sanctuary on an island can be wiped out by a oil tanker disaster; that penguins in the Antarctic are threatened by DDT poisoning; that ancient forests such as the Black Forest are being destroyed by acid rain from the industrial areas of Europe - all these broke the old model of species conservation. The shock was to realise quite how much fundamental damage we had done and are doing to the essentials of life on earth. That was when the environmental movement changed from being concerned with being kind to animals - something found in virtually all faiths as a 'good idea' - to be apocalyptic. It began to see that looking at single species - such as the tiger in India or the oryx in Arabia - was meaningless if their habitats were likely to be wiped out by rising sea-levels, global warming, acid rain or population demands.

So report after report churns out, using "end of the world as we know it" language. The big question becomes how can we motivate people to change in time. By default, one model emerges - constrain people. Legislate for them, for their own good. For, so the argument goes, we know what is necessary for the long term well being of the environment. So let us make sure people are constrained to act properly. An example of this thinking would be the placing of electrified barbed wire around game reserves in places like Kenya. That way the hungry, dispossessed 'natives' will learn not to invade lands which originally belonged to them.

This legislative dimension finds it echoes in many of the millenarian movements of Europe - from the edicts of Savonarola to the promulgations of the New World Puritans. There is a powerful legacy of imperialism and racism, which sometimes shades into a form of fascism, in certain quarters of the environmental movement. The reverse side of this is a silly utopianism, which ignores the harsh physical realities and drifts off into spiritualisations of the problem. Much of the so called New Age thinking fails to grasp the old problems of sin, wickedness and power. They picture us as simple folks who have been misled and if only we can 'return to nature' all will be solved. So a great romanticisation of native peoples takes place which helps no-one. However, those sections of the New Age which do grapple with these wider issues, which do look seriously at the question of human nature and of 'sin', offer some of the most fascinating and thought-provoking ideas currently around.

Alongside these outlooks has arisen the "enlightened self-interest" model. This bases its hopes for change upon appealing to self-interest. Let us not pollute the seas, or we shall not be able to go swimming on our holidays. Don't cut down the rain forests because we don't yet know what useful plants and animals for medicine there might be there. Here is a classic one from a recent fact sheet on Wetlands, called, jokingly, "Liquid Assets"!

"In the South-eastern USA, trappers and landowners in Louisiana received US$24.1 million in 1976-77 from the sale of pelts of which 85% were harvested from wetlands. Major species harvested were nutria, muskrat, mink, racoon and river otter. This harvest supplements income in rural areas and provides off-season employment to groups such as agricultural workers and commercial fishermen."

This appeal to human self-interest and profit is also failing. In fact it has backfired. For it leaves unquestioned the assumption of a constantly increasing GNP which quite simply the world cannot sustain. Put even more bluntly, the USA (or indeed Europe) is a luxury the world cannot afford! Furthermore, who decides what are legitimate national self-interests. The Brazilians say that they cannot afford not to destroy the rain forests because their people need land. Poverty and injustice combined with the multi-national ranching business is what is primarily destroying the Amazon. The poverty of the poor of Brazil cries out for justice. The cattle rancher's produce goes to feed the fast-food economy of the USA. Yet it is not the North Americans who are being asked to change, but the Brazilians!

In appealing to self-interest, the environmental movement has fused self-interest with apocalypse. We are warned that unless we do take more care, we will destroy the world and then no-one will have central heating, or cars or fast food - or even universities! It is, we are told, in our own interest to avert the End. Yet the very forces upon which conservation seeks to build its programme for change - self interest and human economic growth - are the very forces which have got us into this mess in the first place. As I have said earlier, the failure of Western civilisation to take seriously the psychological consequences of the Copernicus Revolution, alongside the physical ones, has led us to a state of mind whereby we equate what we want and need with the ultimate purpose of creation. Again, the Orthodox put it clearly.

> 'We must return to a proper relationship with the Creator AND the creation. This may well mean that just as a shepherd will in times of greatest hazard, lay down his life for his flock, so human beings may need to forego part of their wants and needs in order that the survival of the natural world can be assured. This is a new situation - a new challenge. It calls for humanity to bear some of the pain of creation as well as to enjoy and celebrate it.'
> (Orthodoxy and the Ecological Crisis - issued by the Patriarchate of Constantinople and the WWF, 1990)

It is into this disturbing mess that religion can shed some light. In 1986, on behalf of the World Wide Fund for Nature (WWF) International, we at ICOREC brought together representatives of the main organisations of the five major religions, along with representatives of the world's major environmental organisations. This happened at Assisi for very obvious reasons. There, the two worlds met and a new alliance was forged establishing a network on conservation and religion. Now, nearly four years on, there are seven faiths formally involved with two more on the way to joining. World wide over 70,000 religious communities or groups are active in ecological action or work, from Swedish Lutheran parishes to Thai wats, from Baha'i Spiritual Assemblies to mosques in Turkey. A great movement of faith. Yet, interesting as this may be, it is the challenge and confrontation which is really exciting.

When WWF invited the faiths, it really wanted them to bless its work, to say what a jolly good job the environmental organisations were doing and then

144

to go home. What actually happened was a major confrontation between the utilitarian, anthropocentric, self-interest, growth model of Western conservation and the diverse philosophies of the faiths. Basically, the five faiths originally involved, Buddhism, Christianity, Hinduism, Islam and Judaism, rejected the utilitarian, anthropocentric model of reality. To this the conservationists also had their challenge. They rightly pointed out that while it may be true that the faiths have wonderful teachings in their scriptures and in their traditions and philosophies, none of the faiths had done much to live out these views or teachings to the improvement of the environment.

Since Assisi the process of learning and of re-evaluating positions and of opening up to other's perspectives has gathered pace. With this opening up comes some hope. Just taking Christianity, a Franciscan Centre for Christian Ecology has been established in the Pontifical University of Rome; the World Council of Churches has at last got round to thinking about the creation part in their Justice, Peace and the Integrity of Creation programmes; an Orthodox Feast Day of Creation has been created and an environmental protection programme is starting with the monasteries on Mount Athos; a new environmental Sunday School scheme has been adopted by all the mainstream churches in Kenya. All these are signs of a shift both in terms of evaluating Christian insights on ecology and of doing something about it.

But the encounter of ecology with Christianity has not been an easy one. For many in the environmental movement, Christianity's emphasis on humanity at the expense of the rest of creation has earned Christianity the label of the environmental arch-baddy! As I have shown, there is some justification for this. The challenge ecology presents to theology is that of being the roots of the enviromental crisis and of the poverty of response. In return, as theology - or to be more accurate, the Churches - increasingly appreciate how salvation history has been distorted, so the faith is better placed to help conservation re-examine its basic working assumptions. Key amongst these must be our place in creation and the limit to our rights of use. The Christian message of metanoia is vital to a world view which sees human behaviour as essentially irredeemable; to a world which has fixed upon the Apocalypse but lacks the insights of Christianity's other vision of the future - the Kingdom of God on earth.

Many in the conservation movements see the future as hopeless. They cannot see any hope and view themselves as writing the longest suicide note in history. Many are angry and crippled by guilt for what we have done as a species. In this context the Christian message of celebration of creation, of purpose beyond ourselves, of repentance and forgiveness are sorely needed and now increasingly being used. In return the conservation movements have awoken action from the beliefs of the Churches and this is also giving rise to hope.

The working relationship between ecology and Christianity is still very new and very tender. The need for internal re-evaluation on both sides is paramount, for without it both conventional ecology and conventional Christianity are not only incapable of helping humanity and the rest of creation out of this crisis - they are actually helping to create and fuel the crisis. We need a new understanding of our place in creation - before there is no creation, or at the least, no "us" to reflect on this.

I began with two men on a mountain. The arrogance of a world view which leads us to climb a vast, millions of years old mountain, and say we have conquered it, would be laughable, were it not so dangerous. The simplicity of a world view which sees us as only a part of creation, is attractive but ultimately I would argue, not realistic about the actual situation we are in. Somehow, if we are to emerge from this crisis of our environment, we need to find a path between these. A path which allows us to take responsibility, but within a greater plan than just human well being.

Notes on the Contributors

Christof K. Biebricher is research scientist at the Max Plank Institute for Biophysical Chemistry in Göttingen, and lecturer in Biophysical Chemistry at the University of Braunschweig.

Luco J. van den Brom is lecturer in the philosophy of religion at the University of Utrecht. His writings include *God Alomtegenwoordig* (Kampen 1982; a revised edition in English will appear soon in this series of *Studies in Philosophical Theology*) and *Creatieve Twijfel* (Kampen 1990).

Vincent Brümmer is professor in the philosophy of religion at the University of Utrecht and director of the Utrecht Research Institute for Theology and Religious Studies (INTEGON). He is also a trustee of the Center for Theological Exploration Inc. in Florida, USA. His writings include *Theology and Philosophical Inquiry* (London 1981), *What are we Doing when we Pray?* (London 1984), and *Speaking of a Personal God* (forthcoming: Cambridge 1992).

Willem B. Drees is staff member of the Interdisciplinary Centre for the Study of Science, Society and Religion (Bezinningscentrum) at the Free University of Amsterdam. His writings include *Beyond the Big Bang: Quantum Cosmologies and God* (La Salle 1990) and *Heelal, mens en God: vragen en gedachten* (Kampen 1991).

Chris J. Isham is professor of theoretical physics at Imperial College, London, with strong side interests in philosophy and the work of C.G. Jung. His publications are mainly in the field of quantum gravity.

Malcolm A. Jeeves is professor of psychology and formerly Vice Principal of the university of St. Andrews. He is a Fellow and currently Vice President of the Royal Society of Edinburgh. His principal research interests are in neuropsychology. He is at present President of the International Neuropsychological Symposium and Editor-in-Chief of *Neuropsychologia*. In addition to his many scientific papers his writings include *The Scientific Enterprise and Christian Faith* (Leicester 1968), *Psychology and Christianity: the view both ways* (Leicester 1973), *Psychology through the eyes of faith* (with David G. Myers, San Francisco 1987), *Mind fields: Reflections on the Science of Mind and Brain* (Sydney 1991).

Cas J. Labuschagne is professor in Old Testament studies at the university of Groningen. His writings include *The Incomparability of YHWH in the Old Testament* (Leiden 1966) and a three volume commentary, *Deuteronomium* (Nijkerk 1987-90).

Martin Palmer is director of the International Consultancy on Religion, Education and Culture (ICOREC) in Manchester, and religious advisor to the World wide Fund for Nature International. His writings include *Genesis or Nemesis - belief, meaning and ecology* (London 1988), *Faith and Nature* (London 1987), *Dancing to Armaggedon* (London 1991) and many environmental liturgies.

Arthur R. Peacocke is former dean of Clare College Cambridge and former director of the Ian Ramsey Centre in Oxford. He is Warden of the Society of Ordained Scientists. His writings include *Science and the Christian Experiment* (London 1971), *Creation and the World of Science* (Oxford 1979), *God and the new Biology* (London 1986), and *Theology for a Scientific Age* (Oxford 1990).

8248